LOVE, DEATH
AND
BEYOND

LOVE, DEATH
AND
BEYOND

A Spiritual Awakening

HELEN ELLWOOD

WINNER OF THE NATIONAL SPIRITUAL WRITING COMPETITION

A record of this publication is available from the British Library.

ISBN 978-1-910027-51-6

Typesetting by Wordzworth Ltd
www.wordzworth.com

Cover design by Titanium Design Ltd
www.titaniumdesign.co.uk

Cover images
by courtesy of Marek Studzinski and Banesa

Published by Local Legend
www.local-legend.co.uk

**LOCAL
LEGEND**

Dedicated to Pat Merriam

Acknowledgements

I thank my parents for encouraging my storytelling, igniting the spark for writing, and all those who helped to broaden my mind and who have patiently advised and encouraged me in the writing of this book: Tony Plato, Kerry Searby, David Halfpenny, Jon Morris, Danielle Betty Parker, Barbara Wolter, Hazel Prior, Richard Talaska, Sarah-Louisa, Eve Blunt, my friends in the Subnanos Writing Group and Nigel Peace at Local Legend.

You all believed in me before I believed in myself.

And this book would not have been written without the love and teaching of my dear pets Timmy, Betty, Hegel and Dolly.

www.local-legend.co.uk

About The Author

Trained as a medical scientist, Helen has also always been a keen spiritual explorer. First embracing Buddhism for its compassionate attitude to all living beings, she then travelled the world with a battered backpack to learn about other cultures and world views.

Despite this, she says, "I was living in fear of death every day and encasing myself in a shell of denial about the spiritual world." With no religious belief, she saw only a terrifying oblivion at the end of this life.

It was Beryl the hamster who changed everything. With a deep love for all animals from an early age, watching Beryl's soul rise from her body at death shocked Helen into opening her mind to the spiritual and the numinous. And then the paranormal experiences came thick and fast.

Having also suffered two serious accidents and disabling illness, not to mention heart failure, some may imagine Helen to have a rather jaundiced attitude to life. But nothing could be further from the truth. In this beautifully written memoir, she writes joyfully and with total honesty.

Every reader will identify with her doubts and fears and be inspired by her gradual understanding, the strength of her belief and the triumph of the human spirit.

Helen's website is *www.helenellwood.com*
and her social media accounts are
@helenellwood on Twitter, ellwood_writes on Instagram
and *https://www.facebook.com/crazyanimalwoman*

The Author's Previous Work

2014: *Message in a Bottle* (a castaway memoir) long-listed for the Mslexia memoir competition.

2014: *The Camp Fire* (science fiction) published in the anthology *After the Fall* (Boo Books).

2017: *Spreading Magic* (a children's fantasy) published in the anthology *Chasing Unicorns* (Swanwick Writers).

Helen has also written scripts for BBC docudramas and her poetry has been published by regional writing groups, her short stories broadcast on radio, and three plays have been staged by amateur theatres.

Contents

ONE

Heart and Soul

"Oh," I said, taking a deep breath and reaching for the back of a chair. "I don't feel quite right."

It was Sunday, Richard and I were about to have lunch together. I'd made a vegetarian shepherd's pie. As I stood to go to the kitchen to start steaming the vegetables, I felt lightheaded. There was a high-pitched ringing in my ears and the world started to move away from me as a sudden pain squeezed my chest. I'd had medical training and guessed what was happening, but the rest of me was struggling to catch up with reality.

"I think I'm having a…"

Richard's face changed from confusion to shock as I crumpled into a heap on the floor.

"Call an ambulance," I gasped.

Are you afraid of dying or worried about where our beloved pets go when they leave us? It's a question that has fascinated humanity since the dawn of time. If you have a religious faith, you may well believe in an afterlife and, because of that, have a degree of courage in the face of your mortality. Others follow their own spiritual path and have their own ideas. But with no belief system, the idea of death can be terrifying for many people – it certainly was for me for many years.

It's natural to be afraid. We're here on this planet for such a short time and then we leave. Like the little ballerina in a musical box, our spring is wound up at the beginning of life and we dance for our allotted span, trying to forget that the mechanism will one day wind down. Instead, we listen to the music and watch the other dancers around us, ignoring the inevitable end.

Then, at an unknown moment, the music stops.

Richard knelt down by me and fumbled with his phone, his fingers skidding over the screen as he tried to get it to work. A detached part of my mind realised that he couldn't unlock it.

"It's not working," he said, a terrible note of panic in his voice. I knew I only had minutes left before losing consciousness.

"Use mine," I whispered, barely able to breathe. "It's in the dining room."

My vision was tunnelling. A lion was squeezing the life out of me. Its claws went deep into my heart and the weight of its body against my chest made me want to throw up. I rested my head on the sofa wondering why Richard was taking so long. The sofa felt soft against my cheek. I closed my eyes.

Finally, I heard him talking to the paramedics. He put them on speaker and they told me to lie on my right side while I waited for them to arrive. I did as I was told and lay down like an old dog. The pain was increasing steadily and I wondered how much more I could bear as I breathed slowly to keep panic at bay.

At last, a man and a woman dressed in green burst into the living room and got me onto the armchair. They sprayed something under my tongue and gave me aspirin to chew.

"All right, sweetheart," the woman said, "we just need to take a trace of your heart. Is that okay?"

I nodded. Electrodes were placed on my chest and I heard machines begin to beep.

"I'm sorry," she said a few seconds later, "you're having a heart attack. We need to get you into hospital as quick as we can."

Is death a dark, empty oblivion, or a place where we all meet up and live happily ever after? Maybe it's a temporary state leading to rebirth. You can understand why people don't talk about this much. It's not a lot of fun. Most of us pretend we're immortal, not because we haven't understood the facts of life, but because facing up to death is simply too uncomfortable. It's much easier to watch TV, keep busy and forget that our lives have an expiry date. I thought my heart was perfectly healthy. I had no idea that it was going to fail.

Yet surely death shouldn't be taboo. If we can learn to talk about it and share our experiences, then maybe our fears can be eased. By sharing my journey from total scepticism to belief, I hope to offer some evidence that there is indeed light and love at the end of the proverbial tunnel. And I'm not talking about religious belief, rather a sense of open-mindedness about the spiritual dimension of life and an understanding that we, and our dear pets, do go on to some kind of afterlife.

Still, it's really hard for us to make sense of the world in moments like this when everything is out of control. We can be travelling along life's pathway one minute, thinking we have a plan and there's plenty of time to do what we want, but then something comes along and wrecks things. We assume our children will grow up to be adults and that we'll all live long and happy lives until we pass away peacefully when we're very old, with our family around us, without pain or sickness. But life rarely works out like that.

As I was being carried along the road to where the ambulance waited, I remembered the young starling. I'd been watching it proudly doing acrobatics with its friends in the sky over my front garden only a week before. Suddenly it took a wrong turn and hit my window at full speed with a shocking crash. It left a dust angel image on the glass: the elegant arc of perfectly symmetrical wings, the head to one side, neck snapped. A ghostly record of that moment when before and after were for a split second superimposed. It had fallen to the ground, flapping and wild-eyed, dragging an outstretched wing in circles like a broken moth. I'd run to rescue it but was too late.

There's something shocking about picking up a dead bird, almost as though we shouldn't touch things that belong to the air. I stroked the feathers back into place and supported the broken neck with my hands as I carried it, still warm, to the back garden. The ground had been too hard to dig a hole, so I'd laid the little body at the foot of a tree and covered it with pine needles and rose petals.

Was this some kind of warning?

I'd been happily enjoying the thermals of conversation with my friend and looking forward to Sunday lunch, when suddenly my heart had failed. And just like the broken bird, I now faced oblivion.

My scientific brain did not believe in 'signs', but sometimes the universe brings things together in mysterious ways. We call these things coincidence or synchronicity, depending on our belief system.

I did have a genuine psychic warning one cold winter's day when I was eight years-old. We didn't have central heating in our house so I was getting dressed by my electric fire and about to run downstairs for breakfast. I didn't bother with my plimsolls, those black, rubber-soled, elasticated shoes children wore in those days. Then suddenly I heard a calm, clear voice in my head.

"Put on your shoes!"

It was a grown-up voice, filled with quiet authority. The words were a command, not a request. Without knowing why, I obeyed, then went to turn off the fire. As I touched the switch, my fingers seemed to stick to it and I couldn't let go. A split-second later, I woke up spread-eagled on the other side of the room with the hairs on my arms standing on end and my hand hurting.

I ran downstairs, feeling very shaky, and told my parents what had happened. My mother held me close while my father turned the electricity off at the mains and ran upstairs to my attic bedroom. He came back down with the fire, his face thunderous with a rage I'd never seen. I watched in shock as he ran into the garden and threw the fire over the wall into the alleyway. As he let it fly, he roared.

I was terrified and began to cry. But my mother told me that he was angry with the fire, not me, and explained that putting on my plimsolls had actually saved my life. The rubber soles had protected me. I might not have understood all her words about electricity and earthing, but I was very glad I'd paid attention to that authoritative voice. This happened twice more, once when there was a snake on the path in front of me and again when a shark was very close to me in the sea – more of that later – and on each occasion the voice clearly and calmly gave me life-saving instructions.

I'm sure many people have this kind of experience. It may not be a voice, but we might get a sudden intuition in our gut that something isn't quite right, even when there doesn't seem to be any reason for it. It's just a feeling. I didn't question it when I was a child. It felt natural and I didn't even tell my parents about it. I just accepted that I'd been told to put my plimsolls on and that had saved my life. Rather than focusing on the voice, I simply went to school the next day and excitedly told the story of how I'd nearly died, and for a few moments I was a celebrity amongst my friends. Then everyone forgot about it.

Now I was nearly dying. As I lay in the ambulance, a paramedic placed a heavy crisscross seatbelt over my chest and inserted a cannula into my arm. I was still in shock, noticing each event in minute detail: how narrow the trolley was, the electrodes attached to my wrists, legs and chest, Richard buckling himself into the spare seat. The paramedic called in on the radio to the hospital, "Sixty year-old female, heart attack, coming in on blue lights."

For the first fifty years of my life, the idea of a Heaven with wild-flower meadows and mountains was meaningless. There were no angels in my vision of the afterlife, no long-lost pets or relatives, no loving God and no plan for humanity. On the other hand, my mind couldn't imagine or cope with pure oblivion and non-being, so I had ended up thinking that I would be whisked away, all alone, into a place of absolute darkness. And there I would stay, without hope of rescue, for eternity. So would everybody else.

I don't know how I came up with this particular Hell and I argued logically about it in my head for years. Surely, I would say to myself, if you're conscious of the darkness and isolation, that means you're self-aware and therefore experiencing some kind of existence. And why would you be the only conscious being? There must be others around, you wouldn't be alone. And why darkness, no sense of touch? Despite trying to be rational about it, my dark idea haunted me for decades.

We are more fortunate these days. Not only do we talk about grief a lot more but, due to the Internet, we can share our spiritual lives with less fear of ridicule. If you search for 'after-death communication' (ADC) or 'near-death experiences' (NDE) on YouTube, you'll find a wealth of videos where utterly credible and sensible people talk about their experiences openly.

I had none of this when I was young. My family lived in two spooky and crumbling farmer's cottages built in 1715, joined together by interconnecting doors. There were ten small rooms in the house and my friends and I used to love playing hide-and-seek, running up and down the spiral staircases and hiding in cupboards. I slept in the attic bedroom with a sloping roof and a little window that looked out onto the street. Halfway up the spiral staircase there was a tiny room containing the water tank. It was a scary room, full of spiders, cobwebs and ghosts. Or so I believed. Every night when I went to bed, I would say a polite "Hello" to the ghosts that lived there thinking that, if I didn't, they might come and get me.

I was glad when I got to my teenage years and moved down to the second floor. My brother went up to the attic where he could play his music. I preferred being there because it was nearer the downstairs bathroom. However, it wasn't as safe as I thought.

One day, I was just entering my bedroom when my files on top of the wardrobe flew across the room. I mean, they really flew, they didn't just slip down by gravity. They hurtled through the air and landed on my bed about eight feet away. I'd heard about poltergeists, although I never thought I'd ever witness one. Thanks to the film *The Exorcist* a lot of people were talking about spooky things and somehow I knew the best thing to do was to show no fear. I paused in the doorway.

"Is that all you can do?" I said. Pretending nonchalance, I then walked into the room and it never happened again.

Activity like this has been reported around the world and across all cultures. According to two scientists who have been studying these phenomena, Pierro Brovetto and Vera Maxia, the one thing they have in common is that, "Poltergeist disturbances often occur in the neighbourhood of a pubescent child or a young woman."

We can all remember the turmoil of our teenage hormones, the spots on the skin and the struggle to find our own identity. There's a lot going on at that time.

They go on to hypothesise that, "The changes in the brain that occur at puberty involve fluctuations in electron activity that, in rare cases, can create disturbances up to a few metres around the outside of the brain."[1] These fluctuations could result in a disturbance at the

---

[1] https://www.newscientist.com/article/ dn13563-theyre-here-the-mechanism-of-poltergeist-activity/

quantum level of reality and so cause an increase in the pressure of the air around them, which, in turn, could cause objects to move. In other words, it's more to do with Physics and the possibility of telekinesis than with any evil spirit or haunting, which is quite a relief.

A few months later, I dreamed that someone was in the room with me. At least, I thought it was a dream. I was petrified. When I saw the figure's face I wanted to scream because there was a beak where the mouth should be and it had evil eyes. Next day, there was a bigger surprise when a girl I only vaguely knew came up to me.

"Were you all right last night?" she asked, straight out. I hesitated and said that yes, I'd been fine. "Are you sure? Did something happen to you at about two in the morning? I sensed something bad happened. Did you have a nightmare?"

I described my dream and she told me that she and her mother had a psychic connection and often communicated telepathically. This was how she had picked up on my experience. It was the first time someone I trusted had told me anything like this so I felt inclined to believe her. The girl had genuinely known I'd had a nightmare that night and we became friends. But I never talked to the other girls about it because they would have ridiculed us.

I was becoming aware that life can be weird around this time because I was also having premonitions. At first I'd assume it was all coincidence, but every time I had a feeling that something bad was going to happen, it did. I would meet the nasty gang of girls that lived on my street or my rabbit would get sick. It always started with a funny feeling in my tummy, a little bit like feeling nervous. Many people get a strange sensation in the pit of their stomachs when something bad is about to happen. Yet I still didn't really question these things. They seemed natural and the premonitions were helpful in avoiding bad experiences because I felt prepared.

Because I was so afraid of being thought crazy, I learned to lock my experiences of the paranormal away in my mind, not telling anyone about them. Instead, I rationalised each one in turn and carried on being terrified of death.

A powerful reason for this was my family's attitude towards the paranormal. Family belief systems can become so much a part of the fabric of our world that we don't even notice them. They operate in the background, colouring everything we see, experience and believe. We don't even think of them as rules or beliefs. They're how things are 'supposed to be' and get handed down like heirlooms which can't be challenged without great inner turmoil. I'm sure many people will agree that old patterns of behaviour are hard to shift.

The paranormal was taboo in my family. Mediums on the TV were a joke and God forbid if any of the family were to say that they'd had premonitions, seen poltergeist activity in their bedroom or heard guiding voices that saved their lives.

My father went to church every Sunday while my mother tagged along for moral support, even though she didn't believe a word of it. Despite their differences, they agreed that my brother and I should have some kind of religious education so we were confirmed at a young age and, for a while, we all went along as a family group.

After a couple of years, my brother and I decided not to go anymore. In particular, I'd grown rather tired of this wrathful male God and all the talk of sin, so I decided to leave it all behind and ride horses instead. That was much more fun.

Yet my sense of being 'different' only intensified as I grew older. I was sensitive and empathic, unable to filter out the enormity of the universe and I didn't have a belief system to comfort me. I kept my existential angst to myself. To the outside world I was a normal, friendly young woman. Even when I was seventeen and falling in love with Tony, my gorgeous Greek god of a boyfriend, I remained alone with my fears. It wasn't just death, I sometimes found the intensity of being alive too much. I felt like some kind of spirit trapped in a flesh suit. Has anyone else felt like that?

Well, I wasn't alone completely. Tony's mother, Pat, a quietly spoken Scottish woman and a spiritual seeker like me, introduced me to the writings of the great Indian gurus and to her Buddhist teacher, a Tibetan Lama, who had escaped from a place called Kham in Tibet when the Chinese invaded.

The first time I began to accept spirituality involved Beryl, a hamster! I was sharing a house with my friend Kerry, whom I'd met at Occupational Therapy training college. We were both now embarking on our new careers in hospitals and easing into our new lives as responsible adults.

Not that we were very responsible. Our landlady didn't allow pets in the house but we'd decided to ignore this and already had a hamster each. Mine was called Killer and hers was Beryl, and we'd also just got a nine week-old ginger kitten called Timmy. What the landlady didn't see, the landlady didn't know about.

For a while, the hamsters were allowed the freedom of the room to run and play each evening, though not together – we didn't want lots of baby hamsters. And when it was Killer's turn to play, Kerry would look after Timmy in her room and vice-versa when it was Beryl's turn. One evening, during Beryl's playtime, Kerry knocked on my door. Her face was pale.

"Beryl's been eating the phone cable," she said. "She's not well. Can you come and see her?"

I shut Timmy in my room and went downstairs.

"She's not moving," Kerry said, her voice barely above a whisper. "Do you think she's okay? She's had a go at the television cable too."

She gently took Beryl from her cage and handed her to me. Beryl's chestnut-brown fur looked dull. I stroked her back gently but there was no response.

"I could try something my brother used on one of his mice once," I said. "It may sound weird, but a little sugar in warm water brought the mouse back from the brink."

Kerry was too upset and went out of the room while I made some sugar water and offered Beryl a little on my finger; but she just lay on the palm of my hand, not moving. After a minute, though, she licked my finger with her tiny tongue, drank a little more and then curled into herself, rocking a little from side to side. She seemed to be in pain and I didn't know what to do so I just held her with both palms, trying to comfort her with my warmth.

Beryl became still. Then, to my utter amazement, her body definitely felt slightly lighter whilst, simultaneously, a puff of golden, hamster-sized mist lifted away from her body and evaporated in front of my eyes. I was stunned. Had I just seen her soul leaving her body? I didn't believe in souls. So what had I seen? I held her a little longer then carried her body upstairs, deciding not to tell Kerry about the floating mist.

"I'm really sorry," I said. "She's gone."

Kerry took her from me and held her tenderly.

"She was only a year old," Kerry murmured, stroking Beryl's fur. "It's dark now. Let's bury her after work tomorrow evening. I'll keep her here for now."

"Can I get you anything? Some chamomile tea?"

Kerry's face crumpled. She shook her head and I could tell she wanted to be left alone.

"If you need me," I said, "come and knock on my door. It's painful to lose a little friend."

As I prepared for bed, I kept thinking about Beryl. At first, I assumed my mind must have been playing tricks, but then decided to look at it from a scientific point of view. Did this vision amount to evidence? Why would I imagine something so whimsical, especially as I didn't believe in souls or in Heaven? It was almost like seeing a cartoon of a soul leaving a body, except that soul was made up of tiny particles of a dark gold, misty dust. It had even been hamster-shaped!

I knew that if this vision were real, the implications were massive. If it was my imagination – after all, it was exhausting working for the NHS and the mind can play all sorts of tricks when you're tired – then I could just let it go. Yet I knew in my deepest heart that it wasn't a trick of the light or the product of a tired brain.

Still, I wasn't ready to embrace the world of Spirit or God or anything like that. That's why I hadn't shared my experience with Kerry. She was a dear friend and perhaps she would have been enthralled with the idea that I'd seen something so amazing. Perhaps I should have been shouting it from the rooftops as proof that even hamsters go to Heaven. But I knew why I didn't, I was still afraid of being ridiculed. Fear of rejection is a powerful motive for many of us.

I was now at a time in my life when I felt a bit more open to exploring death and what it might mean. My mother's cancer had returned and I knew it was just a matter of time. My father had Parkinson's as well as a heart condition. I was terrified of losing them.

Whenever I had a day off I started going to the library and taking out anything I could find to do with travel and personal spiritual journeys. I wanted to be told by somebody that everything's okay, that my mother would be safe and that I would be too. I wanted to come out of this dark space, this fear. Like so many of us when faced with the fact of mortality, I wanted something to believe in.

Something that really helped was keeping a journal. I wrote down quotes from some of my deep and meaningful books and words of wisdom from spiritual teachers like the Dalai Lama. Sometimes I would write down song lyrics, favourite poems or things that friends and family said that were funny or meaningful. Whenever I felt low or anxious, I'd read some of the entries. The deeply wise people of this world leave us gems that provide comfort when we need it. Yet although the books were inspiring, I didn't really understand the wisdoms they contained. I needed something more concrete to shift my inherited belief system and rewire my attitudes. Beryl's soul journey was a start.

As the ambulance hurtled towards the hospital, I pushed my fear of death to one side. I'd learned to look with more than my eyes, listen with more than my ears and had finally accepted that paranormal events really do happen. Not only that, but that they happen to a lot of people. This book explores the gradual unfolding of my spiritual awareness and documents the evidence that eventually helped me face my mortality with increased courage and hope.

TWO

This Fragile Life

Shortly after Beryl's death, I went down to Devon to visit Tony. We'd remained very good friends after the relationship ended a couple of years before. We drank some tea together, catching up with our news.

"How's your mother getting on?" asked Tony. "She's really sick isn't she?"

"Yes. I don't think the chemotherapy is working."

"That's horrible," he said. "She's an amazing woman." He paused for a second before continuing. "Did you know that my mother knows a nun at Dharmsala, where the Dalai Lama lives?"

I nodded. "Yes, I knitted her a cardigan last year."

"Mum told this nun about your mother and the nun told the Dalai Lama."

"Wow."

I couldn't believe what I was hearing. For me, the Dalai Lama was an enlightened Yoda-like figure. He shook the hands of royalty and sat on a throne, offering ancient and deep wisdom to the world – an inscrutable man of infinite wisdom, representing a culture I didn't understand. He was on a level with the Pope for goodness' sake. And now he knew about my mother!

"Once he knew," continued Tony, "he and the whole nunnery prayed that your mother wouldn't suffer and would have a happy rebirth."

I didn't know what to say. Tears came to my eyes. I didn't want to begin grieving in front of him in case he hugged me and then I would never be able to let him go. Instead, I excused myself and went down to the bottom of the garden where a little brook trickled over pebbles. I didn't believe in the power of prayer but, you know what, that didn't matter a scrap. The Dalai Lama had prayed for my dear, wise mother.

Sometimes it feels like the universe is nudging us in a specific direction. Things keep happening to show you a certain pathway. It's like you're walking through a forest with all sorts of tracks going this way and that, and you see lights in the distance. You're drawn to those lights and so you wander off your normal, well-trodden track onto paths unknown. Or maybe you ignore the signs and carry on, but then a beautiful deer turns up in a dappled clearing to your right and you feel you should go that way. Sometimes it takes courage to follow the signs and sometimes it feels like the most natural thing in the world.

I'd been interested in Buddhism ever since I met Tony's mother but had only read a little bit about it. Now the Dalai Lama of all people was praying for my mother. I couldn't wait to get home to tell her. Was the universe nudging me in this direction? I imagined all the maroon-clad nuns in the Himalayan village of Dharmsala, and the Dalai Lama himself, praying for my mother's happy reincarnation. I could imagine the chanting echoing over the mountains, carried by the wind.

Have you ever had one of those moments when time seems to stand still and where everything around you feels special somehow? It can happen when we're looking at a sunset or sitting by a campfire.

You get a sense of magic in the air and, although things aren't always right with the world, you feel at peace for that moment.

As I sat there looking at the pebbles, I felt completely calm. My tears subsided. Sunlight filtered through the leaves of the trees by the brook. For the first time in my life, I actually listened to the water properly. I really heard it. I hadn't taken the time to listen before and now understood why poets talk of water chuckling over pebbles. It was a moment outside time, suffused with a strange light.

As soon as I got home, I went to the living room to call my mother on the house phone. Timmy followed me and began to attack the coiled phone cable as I dialled.

"Hi, Mummy," I said as soon as she answered. She didn't like being called Mum.

"Hello dear. How did you get on in Devon?" she asked. Her voice sounded tired. She was always softly spoken but today she sounded distant.

"I had a wonderful time. And I've got some crazy news."

"Do tell."

When I told her about the Dalai Lama praying for her, she laughed in disbelief.

"That's incredible! Well, goodness me, I'm tickled pink."

"That's like being prayed for by the Archbishop of Canterbury," I said and she laughed again.

"Please thank Tony's mother for me, it was very sweet of her."

Despite this wonderful, shared moment, I could feel myself falling down the black hole of the future. Death wasn't academic anymore. My mother really was about to go on that terrifying journey.

I thought back over my life to see if I could find further evidence to support life after death. Like Thomas in the Bible, some of us need to see the actual wounds before we really believe anything. I don't know why seeing Beryl's soul lift up like that hadn't had a bigger effect on me. If it was my fear of breaking the taboo of becoming a spiritual person, then what would it take to make me change my mind?

One event that came to mind was a brief out-of-body experience (OBE) I'd had when I was sixteen. One frosty day, Tommy the pony and I had been cantering and trotting in gentle figures of eight on a clear patch of grass in Bushy Park, London. I was busy training him for one of my mother's speech therapy patients. His wealthy parents had bought the pony to see if it would help their son with his cerebral palsy but, although Tommy was good-natured, he was easily spooked and pretty wild. The boy was unable to go near him so I had been drafted in to help Tommy learn to trust again. My parents couldn't afford to buy me a horse and this arrangement meant I could ride every weekend for free, so I was happy.

I told Tommy's owner that I was going for a little run and I would be back soon. I'd trained Tommy to voice commands, so all I had to do was lean forward and whisper, "Go!" The wind whipped past my face. I glanced down. Tommy's legs were a blur. For those few moments, I felt free and truly alive. Then I saw rough ground ahead and we needed to turn or risk a broken leg.

Having read *Black Beauty* as a child, I was always gentle with horses, never pulling on the bit or kicking them with my legs. I gave the signal to turn – we just had time – but Tommy tossed his head and carried on at full speed.

"Woah!" I yelled, leaning back and putting firmer pressure on the reins. He fly-bucked, all four hooves in the air, his back arched up like a rodeo horse, slamming through my spine. The elastic of my riding hat snapped with the force of the whiplash and the hat flew from my head. Tommy landed and charged forward, hardly breaking stride.

"Woah, Tommy. Woah!"

I pulled harder, but his neck felt as strong and inflexible as a concrete pillar. He'd got the bit between his teeth. I see-sawed the reins to get contact. Tommy fly-bucked a second time. As he landed and surged forward, I sat back, legs long, to regain my balance. Without my hat, a fall was unthinkable and I had to stay on, I had no choice. I was a good rider, able to sit to almost anything but despite all my experience I felt myself slip.

My body fell forward down Tommy's shoulder headfirst. Simultaneously, the conscious part of me, the bit that I think of as me, pulled up and away, shouting a silent "No!" I reunited with my body just before my head made contact with the frosty ground.

Many people have OBEs especially if they have a near-death experience. They see themselves floating up and away from their body and can often describe things that are happening to them. I didn't float away exactly, it's more like I yanked myself backwards.

There is no scientific evidence that our consciousness can survive outside the body, yet it's an experience that's been reported many times. The medical world believes that the experience is a reaction to severe stress and that it comes from a disturbance in the areas of the brain responsible for processing visual information. This doesn't seem to match many of the reports from people who have left their bodies and witnessed their own resuscitation or seen a tunnel and a light beyond.

I wanted the medical explanation to be wrong.

I heard Tommy's hooves thundering back towards me, then I smelled his hay-scented breath on my face. I couldn't move a muscle or see. There was simply the sound of horse breath. Then I felt Tommy's huge tongue lick me from my chin to my forehead and my body took an enormous gasp of air, the first since I'd landed.

My sight began to return as a shadow fell over me, Tommy's owner. Hands reached down and grabbed the lapels of my coat, pulling me to my feet.

"You're going to be all right!" he shouted, holding me upright like a rag doll with my toes skimming the ground, my head flopping forward. "You're all right."

My feet looked funny, like those of a puppet with broken strings. He tried to get me to stand by repeatedly lowering my feet to the ground, expecting my legs and spine to co-operate. He shook me and my head flopped back and forward.

"You're all right. Come on, stand. Put your feet on the ground," he insisted.

There was just a tiny tingle in my toes. My feet resting on the ground, I became aware of my knees and calves although my head was still flopped forward and my arms hung down, useless.

"That's it. Stand. You can do it."

He was still holding me up but my legs felt rubbery, empty and hollow. He helped me to a nearby bench and gently sat me down. After a while, I became aware of my torso and my back. I could move my arms weakly and lift my head. There was still no pain, no fear, no speech. I was a calm, passive observer.

Once I was sitting on the bench unaided, he asked if I could ride home. I nodded. When you're sixteen you think you can do anything. He lifted me onto Tommy's saddle where I slumped like a sack of coal. Tommy stood very still. Normally, he skittered sideways at the slightest noise and pawed the ground, keen to run. My weak arms reached to hold on to his mane. I spoke, my lips and tongue alien.

"Home, Tommy. Go home."

He moved forward gently, looking after me, with just the flicker of his ears betraying his anxiety. I'm sure we've all met animals like Tommy. Guardian angels with fur. It was the first time an animal had taken care of me. Although he was a very nervous horse, he made sure I got home safely. I told my parents I'd had a bit of a fall but I didn't tell them how bad it was because I was afraid they may never let me ride again if they knew the truth. My mother put a board under my mattress to ease my backache. Once the delayed concussion had resolved, I was riding Tommy again in the park.

I was to learn many years later that I'd broken my back and neck that day. I was told by a spinal specialist that I would have been in neural shock and that the terrible First Aid I'd received had re-engaged my nervous system. Tommy's kiss had got me breathing. If Tommy's owner had called an ambulance and kept me still on the ground, my chances of survival would have been very slim. Mobile phones hadn't been invented so it would have taken time to call for help and then the ambulance would have struggled to get across the rough ground to me.

I'm not recommending that you shake anyone who falls from a horse. It's an appalling thing to do. However, on this occasion, it worked. Although I owe my ability to move to that man, I owe my life to Tommy. Without his big, slobbery kiss that got me breathing, I would certainly have died.

I thought about that moment when I refused to fall. I remembered pulling backwards and upwards briefly. I could see everything as if from just above my right shoulder. It only lasted a split second. What had happened? If I'd really split off from myself, it would imply a separate soul. And that would mean the possibility of an afterlife.

Thinking of further evidence, I remembered the calm, parental voice I'd heard when I was eight before I touched that electric fire. I'd heard it again when I was walking along with my family on holiday. We were all in single file and I was in front. It was one of the long hot summer days of the early Seventies, when the grass in August grew brittle, dry and gold. We were walking along a narrow track on the South Downs. Bracken grew high to either side and the sun was beating down on our heads. My cousins and I had been warned about the dangers of adders in the area and we'd all learned about the tell-tale diamond pattern running down their backs.

I was enjoying the walk and looking forward to our picnic when suddenly I heard that same clear voice in my mind simply telling me to stop. So I stopped. I didn't see anything at first but when the others caught up with me I saw the snake. It was well camouflaged, about three feet ahead. Two more steps and I would have stepped very close or even onto it. That's when most adders bite.

In an emergency, our eyes send a reflex visual message direct to the fight-or-flight response area of the brain before we're consciously aware of it. It's like when you put your hand too near something hot, when the pain receptors send a reflex message to pull your hand away. I might have seen the adder in this way with my brain processing the image a few seconds later. But I don't think that's what happened.

I heard the same voice another time when I was an adult, during a visit to Micronesia. I was carrying a bamboo fishing pole and wading into the sea to catch fish when the voice said, "Stop where you are." I felt slightly foolish standing knee-deep when normally I would have waded out up to my waist but, moments later, a shark swam towards me. It slowed as it approached and just as it came level with me it rolled onto its side slightly and looked me right in the eye. I could see every detail of its skin, gills and fins, a beautiful reef shark about four feet long. I stayed very still as I'd been taught and, as it swam languidly away from me, I backed up carefully and got onto dry land. If I'd waded in any deeper, the shark would have cut me off from the beach. And if it had been hungry, it could have bitten me.

There would have been no time for calm voices to tell me to act a certain way. If I'd seen the snake or shark in my peripheral vision, I would simply have frozen in place without knowing why, or moved away before any thoughts had time to surface. In a reflex, there's no time for a quiet, parental voice with clear guiding words – especially a voice containing deep wisdom and authority.

Even while writing this book, I had another warning. I was walking in the High Street on my way to a food shop and had a choice of going left, the long way round, or straight ahead. There was nothing to show any alarm either way and it would have been unusual to take the left-hand route as it was quite a bit further.

The guiding voice told me to turn left, suggesting that there was danger straight ahead. I paused, almost tempted to argue that I couldn't see anything dangerous. However, I took the advice and went left. As I rounded the corner and walked back towards the shop, a commotion was happening where I would have been if I'd taken the shorter route. Men were shouting aggressively, brewing for a full-on fight in the street. People were coming out of pubs to see what was going on. If I'd ignored the guidance, I would have been right in the middle of the conflict and that would have been dangerous for my heart.

Because of these experiences I'm beginning to believe that we all have 'guardians' or 'guides' who protect us from unnecessary harm. However, they don't protect us from everything and that leaves me puzzled. Why wasn't I warned about the horse accident? Maybe I was warned but didn't listen! We need to learn to listen and respond if we get those little nudges, those intuitions. We all get them. They come in different forms for different people but, if we get any inkling that the road ahead is dangerous, it's wise to pause.

"How are you feeling?" I asked my mother.

"The drugs are helping with the pain a bit but I keep being sick. It's not much fun. But I'm looking forward to your visit."

"So am I." I tried to inject cheerfulness and energy into my voice.

As soon as the conversation was over, my heart sank. I'd been holding onto a vague hope that the current round of treatment might put her in remission. But that hope was growing fainter.

My mother's life hit a wall in 1973. She was young and fit and loved her job, she was enjoying watching her children grow up and had a happy relationship with my father. She loved working in the garden and was even starting a huge project digging out the cellar to turn it into a little museum where she could store the antiques she like to collect.

The chances of getting cancer are now about one-in-two. This is horrific. Only a few years ago, it was one-in-three. In my mother's day, getting breast cancer wasn't at all common but sadly it was often a death sentence. Nowadays, we can gather with our friends and wear pink and run in the park to raise money to fight this horrid disease. The collective experience helps us cope somehow, we feel we're part of something and have hope of a cure. Also, medicine has improved so much since the Seventies. There was little hope for my mother, though. One day she went for a check-up and then she was in hospital, only forty-seven years-old.

While she was recovering from surgery, I took on the responsibility of looking after the family. In those days women were expected to do all the domestic chores so it didn't occur to me that it wasn't my job, as a fifteen year-old girl, to cook and clean in place of my mother. I didn't think for a moment that my father and brother were being lazy; they probably thought I was enjoying taking care of everything.

I soldiered on for a few days until I broke down in tears at school. The teacher took me out of the class, asked what was going on and gave me a cuddle. The school must have had a word with my father because then we all began to work together to keep ourselves going while we waited for my mother to come home. Fortunately, she came through and I put the trauma aside as best I could and concentrated on my O Levels.

Then a year later my father had a heart attack and had a pacemaker fitted. Hearing the news was like being punched in the stomach. I just sat there, staring at the floor, trying to understand. He recovered well but began to have difficulty finding words for things. We'd sit at the dinner table and he'd say, "Pass the… um… the…" then he'd get annoyed and say, "Oh, you know, the whatsit."

At first this seemed the sort of thing that could happen to anyone, but pretty soon it became alarming, especially combined with his hand tremor. As we often did, we made light of it so that we could all cope, whilst in the depths of our hearts we knew we were facing something ghastly. When my parents had retired to the countryside, we'd enjoyed going to church fêtes, eating cream teas and going for walks by Rutland Water together. But my father was soon too shaky on his feet due to Parkinson's Disease to join us, although he still attended church every week as the churchwarden and liked to sit in the garden admiring the roses.

Fortunately, my mother lived another fifteen years before the cancer caught up with her again. She even gave talks to doctors and nurses about the power of positive thinking. We take it for granted now that a healthy attitude to life, good food and plenty of exercise have a beneficial effect on our health but, in those days, the idea of one's diet or mindset making any difference was not widely accepted by the medical world.

Mother and I still went for walks, often getting the giggles if we got lost in the woods. She had trained as a Speech Therapist at the London School of Speech and Drama in her youth. She was a passionate woman, deeply fond of poetry and music, and would often slip effortlessly into role-play. If she tripped up when out with me in the countryside, she'd say, in a 1940s' clipped English accent, "You go ahead without me, Carruthers, I'll only hold you back."

I'd reply something like, "No, I can't leave you here. I shall carry you if I have to but, by gad, I'll get you home.'

We had such fun. Yet that stiff upper lip was real. Even when the cancer had eaten her and left her empty, she was as strong as a wartime hero. But this time, it wasn't a game.

THREE

A Simple Ending

Using words to express love wasn't done in my family. Certainly, there were gifts and actions, such as a warm scarf on the radiator in the morning, breakfast in bed for my mother on Mother's Day, sweets and playfulness on our childhood walks. We shared silly phrases. I knew I was loved and never doubted it, but I never heard those special words.

I was different, I liked to express affection in words and this discrepancy became a problem when my mother was nearing the end. I wanted to tell her how much I loved and appreciated her yet knew that this was likely to be embarrassing for her. I was studying psychotherapy at the time so decided to run this past my tutor.

"What would be the worst that could happen?" he asked.

"She might feel embarrassed."

"Do you think she would feel moved despite the embarrassment?"

"Yes."

"How much do you need to do this?"

"Massively."

So one day, when she was still healthy enough to look after herself, I approached her. She was still young, just turned sixty. We were in the kitchen preparing a simple lunch together while my father was asleep in the front room.

"I've got something awkward to say." My heart was going fast because I didn't want to upset her. "I need to say it, though, so I'm really sorry if this is awkward for you."

She turned to me from the washing up, her head tipped on one side and a dishcloth in her hand, probably guessing what was coming.

"I need to tell you just how much I'm going to miss you," I continued. She turned away and began wiping down the sink and draining board. "I want to tell you how much I love you." My lips were quivering and I could feel tears filling my eyes but carried on with a wobbling voice, "I love you so much. I want to thank you for everything. I'll miss you every day for the rest of my life."

Then my voice failed me.

Even though she'd been wiping the draining board, over and over, I knew she was listening to every word with her heart and soul. She paused, cloth in hand, and turned to me.

"Thank you," she said. "Thank you for saying that. It must have taken a lot of courage."

It shouldn't be embarrassing to tell someone you love them, should it? The trouble is, we all have different ways of expressing affection. It's said that there are five languages of love: gifts, words, the giving of your time, helping people out and physical touch. Just because someone doesn't ask if you need any shopping and doesn't bring you flowers every week, it doesn't mean they don't love you. Just because they can't actually say, "I love you", it doesn't mean they wouldn't step in front of a bus to save you.

I could see she was genuinely touched. I leaned against the fridge, feeling my cheeks tremble uncontrollably yet so glad I took that chance.

It made all the difference later. After that, I reverted to using actions like the rest of the family did to show love.

My mother's choir was going to perform *The Dream of Gerontius*. She wasn't well enough to sing but had bought tickets so we could be in the audience together. That weekend, I left Timmy in Kerry's capable hands and drove to my parents' house. After a catch up over lunch, my mother asked if I would help put fresh sheets on the beds. These tasks were now hard for her and I knew we would soon need to consider home-help. As we began, her face became serious and I could tell she was going to give me bad news.

"The cancer has spread even further," she said. "It's gone to my lymph system and I won't be able to fight it this time."

My legs went weak. I swallowed.

"I don't know how long I've got," she continued. "There's nothing that can be done now." We paused in our work, pillows all over the floor, duvets scattered. I nodded. I had no idea what to say. "I want you to make me a promise," she said. "When I'm gone—"

At those words, my mind went into a kind of whiteout.

"—if Daddy can't cope alone, find a home for him near to where you live so that you can visit regularly. Don't take him to live with you, it wouldn't work."

What I wanted to do was fall to my knees and beg the universe to spare her. Instead, I told her I would look after him to the best of my ability and that I would heed her advice. She began making the bed again so I stuffed a pillow into its case and helped her straighten the sheet.

"Are you afraid of dying?" I asked.

"Actually, no. There can't be any suffering after you're dead because you're not there anymore. It's simply an ending."

Simply an ending.

That was the bit I couldn't deal with. It wasn't just the concept of the ending of the lifelong relationship with my mother, guardian and best friend. It was the concept of consciousness itself ending. I admired her courage but I didn't understand how she could face oblivion with such calm. She was a deeply wise soul who accepted her non-being with grace. I couldn't, I felt sick.

"I'm a little envious of you," she went on, "with your interest in Buddhism. I'm pleased you're engaging with one of the Big Four. Did you say there's a retreat centre near you?"

"Yes, I'm going next year. Tony's mother told me there's going to be a Tibetan New Year event there so I thought I'd go along."

"It still makes me chuckle to know the Dalai Lama prayed for me."

I hadn't really chosen Buddhism exactly, in fact if anything it looked like it had chosen me. I'd fallen into it somehow through reading so much on the subject and meeting Lama Chime Rinpoche at Pat's house when I was younger. The truth is, like many people, I didn't really know where I was going.

That evening, we went to the concert. Although it was sad that she was too ill to perform that night, I was glad we could sit next to each other and enjoy the music. I was reminded of when she took me to hear my first orchestra when I was ten. The velvet sound of violins and flutes had bewitched me and I still remember how the bass notes of the timpani shook the floor. Now, we were side by side again as the strings began the sombre and melancholic introduction. I was vaguely familiar with the piece but had never really listened to the lyrics before so, when the soloist stood up to sing the part of Gerontius, I was shaken.

> *'Tis death … 'tis he!*
> *As though my very being had given way,*
> *as though I was no more a substance now…*
> *but must needs decay*
> *and drop from out the universal frame*
> *into that shapeless, scopeless, blank abyss,*
> *that utter nothingness, of which I came.*

I shuddered hearing these words and cast a quick, sideways glance at my mother. Her face was relaxed, attentive.

> *Another marvel: someone has me fast*
> *within his ample palm…*
> *a uniform and gentle pressure tells me I am not*
> *self-moving, but borne forward on my way.*

Another soloist, the angel, stood up to sing.

> *My work is done, my task is o'er,*
> *so I come, taking it home…*
> *My father gave in charge to me*
> *this child of Earth e'en from its birth*
> *to serve and save.*
> *Alleluia, and saved is he.*

"Wouldn't it be nice," my mother whispered, leaning towards me, "if all this were true? If angels carried you to a lovely place."

Most of us, unfortunately, have had experience of catastrophic and crushing grief. I wonder if it's easier to bear if the person you're losing shares the same faith. Most cultures in the world have some concept of an afterlife. We tend to believe in some kind of future, whether we're religious or not, because to believe in nothing is almost impossible. Can you imagine non-being? Simply not being aware? It's so much easier to believe in some kind of continuation.

I was too choked up to answer my mother so I just nodded with tears trickling down my face. I had no idea how she was able to face heading off into nowhere with complete acceptance. She believed in nothing: no God, no afterlife, no pretty angels holding people's hands. She didn't believe in rebirth either.

31

And I couldn't believe how courageous she was. I was too attached to my self, to my ego and my identity. The thought of non-being petrified me yet she accepted it with grace. I'd always been impressed by her. Now, as she approached the end of her days on Earth, I was in total awe of her calm state of mind.

A couple of weeks later, my cute and crazy albino hamster, Killer, joined Beryl on that strangest of journeys. He'd been completely fine the day before, climbing up the curtains and sitting on my shoulder as usual. When I checked the next day, he was curled up gently as if in sleep. There was no sign of suffering. No magical mist experience this time, just a dear, dead friend. I was glad he hadn't suffered an injury from all his extreme sports or been eaten by Timmy. He'd lived three long, active years and gone peacefully in his sleep as an old gentleman should.

I placed him in an egg box with the lid open, surrounded by fresh bedding for the rest of that day, just in case he was hibernating. But he wasn't. Kerry and I buried him near Beryl under the winter jasmine.

I continued to visit my parents regularly. My mother's health seemed stable for the moment although I could see she was in pain, but my father's tremor was worse. We made the best of it and shared joyful moments like getting ice cream cones with flakes on top and taking trips out in my car to see the spring lambs. On one of these occasions, I was driving my mother into the countryside for a bit of fresh air while my father stayed at home. She told me that the cancer was now in her mouth and that she was finding it difficult to talk clearly. She gave a hollow laugh.

"Seems a bit ironic doesn't it, with me, a Speech Therapist, struggling to speak?" My face twitched in an attempt to smile. "Is everything going okay for you?" she continued.

"Well…" I hesitated. "Apart from… all this, I suppose so, yes. Life is fine. Kind of. But I'm worried sick about you."

"But you'll be all right, won't you? In the bigger scheme of things?"

"I guess so. In fact, I think I might have met someone, a potential boyfriend."

"How lovely."

My mother had a gentle smile on her face. She seemed to relax, knowing that my life would go on and that I'd have love and companionship just as she'd had. But I didn't want to talk about my possible boyfriend. I wanted to stop the car. Actually, I wanted to stop the universe.

Matt, the possible in question, was a friend of my neighbours. After three months of reading poetry and walking in the countryside together, we both moved further north to be nearer my parents. I got a mortgage on a tiny terraced house about an hour's drive away from them and a job at a mental health centre. Matt got a place at a local university to study. Another good thing about this change was that Kerry said she was happy for me to have sole ownership of Timmy.

It was so much easier being closer to my parents. I was able to visit them regularly, my brother came up whenever he could and we had Christmas in London with him that year. Despite clearly struggling, my mother still poured hot brandy on the Christmas pudding and set light to it, just as she had in the old, happy days.

The following February, I went to the local Buddhist centre for the first time. They were celebrating Tibetan New Year and there were going to be some lectures on Buddhism. I'd been reading a lot of books but I thought that actually going there and learning directly would be better. Also, it was going to be nice to meet Lama Chime Rinpoche again.

The night before, I had a vivid dream in which I arrived so late that everyone was already enjoying the evening meal by the time I got there. To prevent this coming true, I set off in plenty of time, but I got lost on the way and arrived late just as in my dream.

Precognitive dreams aren't yet accepted by science, even though there are some well documented cases. For example, Carl Jung claimed to have a dream that predicted his own mother's death[2] and Abraham Lincoln is said to have dreamed of his own death ten days before his assassination. Can you imagine having a dream like that?

Perhaps we really can see the future… Author and neuroscientist, Sidarta Ribeiro PhD, has an interesting take on precognitive dreams. He thinks the dreaming mind projects different scenarios of possible futures, many of which we don't remember; but if one of those scenarios turns out to be accurate, we then may consider it to be precognitive. So in the case of Carl Jung, maybe his mother was getting old and he was unconsciously worried about her.

My mind might have been projecting some kind of anxiety about being late, but that wouldn't explain my feeling of almost reliving my dream when I saw it in reality. Research in this field could change the way we look at our dream lives, the nature of cause and effect and whether time is as linear as we assume.[3]

When I walked into that Buddhist centre, the smell of the incense, the deep colour of the walls and the paintings of the Buddha felt so familiar. My friend Barbara, whom I was due to meet there, was also strongly drawn to the Tibetan culture and had even started learning the language. Had we both been there in past lives? Many people feel drawn to other cultures. Two friends of mine have been pulled towards studying and reading all about Egypt, whilst others feel an affinity for Japan or France.

When I was a child, the first pictures I drew were of strange beasts with horns and spines down their backs and when I got older I loved

---

[2] https://jungiancenter.org/jungs-prophetic-visions/
[3] *Spirit Revelations* (Nigel Peace, Local Legend) has more than a hundred examples of proven precognitive dreams and synchronicities

to draw oriental dragons. Were these drawings my attempts at remembering something I'd seen before? I also loved Japanese prints and costume, Chinese paintings and movies and, when I was travelling in Kathmandu, I remember standing in the main square and somehow knowing that 'home' was just over the mountains. That region was Tibet.

Putting these thoughts to one side, I rushed to the dining room to meet Barbara. Just as I'd seen in my dream the night before, people were sitting at trestle tables eating their evening meal and looking up at me as I walked in. This gave the evening an even stronger air of surrealism.

Lama Chime Rinpoche spent the morning telling us the basic ideas of Buddhism. At one point, he noticed me and shot me a smile of recognition, making me feel I'd made the right decision to come. He told lots of parables in which compassion seemed to be the chief message and then went on to discuss rainbows after death.

He said that deeply enlightened masters who die in meditation are left for a few days before their body is moved. During that time, rainbows can be seen emanating from the body. After that, they are said to exist in a body of light. I lapped all this up in a kind of fairytale way, not taking any of it literally at the time.

However, it turns out that many people see rainbows after losing a friend, relative or beloved pet. There does seem to be some connection, or is it just a myth? We often say it's a sign that all is well, especially with pets. We say they've gone over the Rainbow Bridge to wait for us. In Japanese culture there is a Floating Bridge of Heaven. Whatever the truth of it, for all of us, a rainbow is a sign of hope, of new beginnings and peace.

When the lecture was over, the lama went upstairs to his room for lunch. I'd been struggling with all these concepts on my own for a long time so I asked the junior monk whether I could join as a proper student. A few hours later, I was told I'd been accepted and was to go and see the lama in the meditation room. Barbara gave me a traditional white scarf, made of a very light weave, a mere wisp of fabric, to offer him as part of the ritual.

I walked into the meditation room feeling excited and a bit lost, a bit like going to see the headteacher at school, or a therapist. Even if they don't mean to, they can make you feel terribly self-conscious and you find yourself on your best behaviour. It can be quite inhibiting. I had no idea what to say even though I'd met him before. I got tongue-tied and shy.

He was sitting on the floor on a cushion looking very solid and composed. He smiled at me as I held out the white scarf. Taking it from me gently, he touched it to his forehead and placed it back around my neck before indicating for me to sit down. I folded my inflexible legs as best I could on my cushion opposite him.

He explained the rules. As a beginner Buddhist, I would be expected to obey eight basic commandments which were very like the Christian ones: no killing, no stealing, no bad language, no chemical intoxication, that sort of thing. I quietly wondered whether I was allowed to have a beer or two on Friday nights. He also explained the concept of the bodhisattva: someone who, having attained enlightenment, voluntarily chooses to forgo salvation and stays on Earth for the benefit of everybody.

He then asked me if I was ready to take my vows.

Vows?!

I hadn't banked on doing that. What was I signing up to? I didn't want to shave my head and wear maroon robes but to my own surprise I said, "Yes."

As I promised to look after all sentient beings for all time and forgo Nirvana, a bit of me felt caught up in the romance of being kind to everyone, whilst the rational part of me realised I'd possibly saddled myself with a massive burden. Up until this crucial moment, all I'd wanted to do was meditate and calm my mind so I hadn't given any credence to the religious aspect of Buddhism before.

"I'm going to talk in Tibetan for a while," he said. "I will be talking to my ancestors."

His voice was low and relaxing, the Tibetan language musical and gentle. I gazed around at all the colours on the walls, red, green, blue, white and gold. The buddha statue was smiling slightly with its eyes almost closed. Then the lama stopped speaking and made eye contact with me.

"When I click my fingers, transmission will take place."

Transmission?!

What was he talking about? Transmission of what? I didn't have time to question it. He talked quietly again for a few seconds and then clicked his fingers. To my astonishment, a pulse of energy, a very faintly visible sphere, radiated from the centre of his being and expanded outwards. The moment this energy touched me, my vision went hazy and I lost my sense of self. I had no idea who or what I was or where my self ended and where his began. It was disorientating and very strange indeed.

The sphere of energy then moved on, spreading through the room and out through the roof and the floor and the walls, no doubt going across the garden and into outer space. He smiled. Reality returned. I was alone again, trapped in my own skin, gaping at him like a goldfish.

Like most British people in awkward situations, I pretended everything was completely normal, as if I had mind-melds with Tibetan lamas every day of the week. I don't think it was just my British reserve though. When something stresses us, we can either run away, fight back or freeze like a mongoose. They play dead when under threat, even to the point of sticking their tongues out. Then, when the threat is over, they get up and carry on. Having been seriously bullied by a really nasty boy at infant school, I'd learned to freeze. I did an emotional version of it in situations like this. Nothing to see here. Move along.

"It's hard to know who is who, isn't it?" he said. The comment filled me with relief because for a moment I'd wondered if I was having a funny turn, but clearly he'd felt it too.

Barbara explained that transmission is the planting of a mental seed in the mind of the recipient to guide them on their way to enlightenment. Although part of me was fascinated by the strange experience, it was clear that another part of me felt a little overwhelmed. If Barbara had simply explained it in words alone, I would have dismissed it as nonsense. But to feel it and see it was another thing altogether and I think, to be honest, it freaked me out a little, which is why I froze and pretended nothing was going on.

Well, if young women during puberty can affect the world with their crazy energy, then why can't highly realised, mentally adept Tibetan lamas as well? What seems like magic to us is science to a higher level being. If we were to go back in time and show our mobile phones to someone in the mediaeval era, we would be branded as witches. Maybe both the mental skills of a Tibetan lama and the book throwing of a teenage girl will, one day, be understood by modern Physics.

The weekend finished with a New Year's celebration in the garden in which all the monks danced around in a circle wearing masks and highly coloured boots. As they did so, it began to snow. Yet again, I felt transported back in time to a strangely familiar world. For a moment, Barbara and I were back in Tibet.

Even though all these events helped me appreciate that we are clearly more than our atoms, the thought of death was still frightening and my old fears were super hard to shake off. In fact, I felt more anxious than ever so I booked to have an individual tutorial with the lama to see why. I explained that I'd felt nervous and a bit unreal since the transmission experience.

"Most of my students have egos that are too strong," he said. "I give them exercises to do to make them more open. But your ego is not strong so you have gone too fast too soon."

I nodded, hoping to understand.

"Imagine life is like a train," he continued. "The initiation ceremony and following meditation is meant to give you an idea of your true nature. You are expected to get off the train for a moment and look at it from the platform, then get back on board. But you got off the train, walked up the footbridge and got to see all the way into the distance. This has unsettled you. It will calm down."

I was pleased to hear the anxiety would pass and that he wasn't going to give me complex exercises or rituals to do. I was to take a more direct path with something he called Mahamudra.

"Everything can be meditation," he said. "Making bread, walking, eating. Just focus on what is happening right now and be present. Breathe and relax. You will be fine."

I had no idea at the time that I was going to come across this method many more times. He gave me a few more instructions and I thanked him and tried not to limp too much as I left the room, having had my legs crossed for so long.

From what I'd understood so far, Buddhists believe that each human being is inherently good. All we have to do is to rid ourselves of the toxic layers of thinking and behaving and of the false ideas we have about reality that keep us from seeing our true nature. This can, in turn, make us more peaceful. I realised that intellectually hearing his words and experientially understanding them were totally different. Apparently, you could get to the point of enlightenment in one lifetime if you worked hard. So, no rush then.

However, even if I were to take a long time to feel at peace, it would still be worth practising meditation with a teacher if it removed my fear of death. And I was glad there was no need for faith in some invisible, wrathful father figure.

Timmy settled onto my lap and I noticed how relaxed she was. I always tended to get uptight and intense about everything. Yes, I needed to live more in the moment like she did. She didn't worry about what it all meant, she just purred. Could I do the same?

FOUR

The Gift of Mice

The summer days faded away and soon it was November. Hawthorn berries sparkled on the hedgerows by the canal and frost lay on my suburban garden. Matt, Timmy and I had been at the new house for one year. If it hadn't been for the dark cloud of my parents' ill-health on the horizon, I would have been happy.

The day after my birthday, I went to visit my parents as usual. My father was sitting in his armchair by the gas fire and my mother was lying on the sofa, clearly in pain. She'd lost a lot of weight and looked swamped by her fluffy jumper. The cancer had her tight in its pincers and even the strong opiates weren't much use. I offered her a massage, which often helped, but this time she shook her head.

"Let's go out," she said. My father looked horrified.

"Darling, you're in no state to go out anywhere."

I could see he wanted to protect her but knew it was important for her to do what she wanted. I was prepared to take her anywhere if it would give her a few moments of joy.

"Let's go to the village pub," she said, pushing herself up from the sofa.

She never went into bars. She'd get giggly after one glass of wine at Christmas. Going to the pub at eleven in the morning on a Saturday was wild. I drove us round the corner to the local pub where we sat outside at a picnic table, tucked up in our warm coats. She shot me a mischievous smile.

"I want to have something I've never had before," she said. "What do you recommend?" I ordered her a Tequila Sunrise. "How about you?" she asked. "Why don't you try something new?"

"Okay," I said, caught up in her mood. "I'll have a Southern Comfort. I've seen people drink it in films."

We sat there like two teenagers bunking off school, giggling and trying our grown-up drinks. My mother's cocktail glowed like a tropical evening, the grenadine a deep red sun at the bottom of the glass, filtering up through the tequila and orange juice. I watched her savour the taste.

For a second, I had a flash of insight as to how our lives could have been if she'd not become ill. I'd always wanted to take her to see the Himalayas. She loved mountaineering when young and I knew how much her spirits would have soared at the sight of those crisp mountains. However, this picnic table in Rutland on a cold November day would have to do for my mother and me right now. This was our adventure.

Some people are more alive on their last days than others are their whole life-long. They teach us how to live the best life we can, even if we have pain. It was clear she didn't want to talk about her illness and didn't want any sentimental farewells either. She wanted to live a full life right up to the end. I was so glad we had that last precious morning because, a week later, she was admitted to the local hospice.

When a someone reaches this point, it's not going to be long. At least, we know the level of care is high and that our loved one isn't going to die in pain or alone. This is quite a blessing in a way. I think it also helps us to begin to accept the truth. Her health went downhill fast. She found it difficult to eat and had lost her appetite completely. My father and I visited her often but we were restricted to visiting hours, which was tricky with my full-time job. My brother travelled up from London whenever he could.

One day, after my mother had been in the hospice for a couple of weeks, I noticed a further decline. She lay flat in bed, making no effort to sit up and greet us. There were no jolly quips about the food. She told us she didn't want any more people coming to visit. Just family now. My legs felt like jelly as I helped her to the toilet, holding her hand as we walked, a hand that had once been strong and capable. I noticed her slim wedding ring and the freckles on her arms. When she was safely back in her bed, my father and I sat nearby and I massaged her hands with some moisturiser. She turned her head on the pillow to look at me.

"Thank you, chickens," she said softly, "you've all been very good."

Was she saying goodbye? I could hardly breathe. I tried to smile, my lips quivering. I had no idea that those were going to be her last words to me.

She turned to look at my father. They gazed into each other's eyes for a long moment, then my father leaned over the bed and kissed her with infinite tenderness. A butterfly kiss filled with decades of love, no words needed. It was a beautiful, agonising moment and one that will stay with me to the end of my days.

I could see she was tired and that it was time to leave so I took my father by the arm to guide him out of the room. As we made our way to the door, my mother met my eye. Her gaze held a lifetime of love, fun and beautiful memories. There was a warning in her look as well, as if to say, "Remember what I said. Look after him, but don't sacrifice yourself."

Even though we know it's coming, it's still impossible to bear. You just want to go back in time or pull your beloved back from the brink. I couldn't do that so I gave her what I hoped was a confident smile; her face relaxed and I knew I'd done the right thing.

I fully intended returning the next morning and staying with her for as long as it took. I wanted to be with her at the end and maybe even tell her once more how much I loved her as she slipped away. But that wasn't to be. After I'd gone to bed that night, I got a call from the hospice telling me that my mother had agreed to an injection that would let her sleep peacefully until she died. They said she would never wake up again.

At first, I had the shocking thought that the nurse was talking about assisted dying, then I remembered that palliative sedation, as this process is called, is sometimes used in hospice settings. People who are terminally ill are sometimes offered a sedative drug to ease their distress and pain, when their symptoms cannot be controlled by any other means. It doesn't hasten death and has nothing to do with euthanasia. Our loved ones are allowed to sleep comfortably in peace, nursed and cared for, until death takes them naturally.

My mother had sometimes said that she would like to die in her sleep. She'd felt it was the least traumatic way to go so I was glad she'd been given her wish. But this kindly voiced yet impersonal phone call from a nurse, telling me that my mother would never wake again, broke something in me. I wished I'd been given the choice to be there before the decision was made. But it was my mother's last independent act. She'd cried for years after her own mother passed and knew how painful this time was going to be for me. I guess she didn't want to make it any worse by asking me to be there.

I clung to Matt with Timmy's weight on my legs as I lay wide-eyed, staring at the light of the streetlamp as it filtered through the curtains. It's weird how we notice silly little details at times like this. We can be utterly distraught and yet notice that there's a cobweb in the corner. For me, I noticed one of the curtain clips had come away and there was a gap at the top. It looked uneven, messy. It needed fixing.

I thought of driving to the hospice but what would be the point? I'd probably crash the car anyway and then my father would have two women to grieve over. I'd go as soon as it was light. Huddled in the dark, I waited for the morning. But there wasn't going to be a morning, just a continuation of these awful moments. The gaping curtains, Timmy's comforting weight on my legs and the pain in my heart.

> Stop all the clocks, cut off the telephone.
> The stars are not wanted now, put out every one.
> Pack up the moon and dismantle the sun.

My mother had read poetry to me all my life. She knew so many by heart and would recite them if I was struggling emotionally, or if we were walking somewhere dramatic like a windswept beach or a snowy hilltop.

> Pour away the ocean and sweep up the wood.
> For nothing now can ever come to any good.

I couldn't even cry. I was locked in a state of shock. I just lay there, listening as Matt's breathing eventually slowed to sleep. At two in the morning they rang again and I ran down to the house phone. She had passed away. I went back to bed and stared into the dark, unable to sleep, my mind blank, unable to process it. She'd gone.

I wanted so much to see my mother, even if it was only in a dream. Many people do dream of their loved ones after they've passed. Sometimes these dreams seem completely real. When I was studying Psychology, it was believed that dreams were just our daytime nonsense being sorted by our brains. But anyone who's dreamed of a relative or pet knows that there has to be more to it than that.

When I was twenty-one, I had a dream about my uncle. I was extremely ill at the time with salmonella poisoning, having spent six months travelling with Tony, and I was staying at his mother's house before making my way home. In the dream my uncle walked towards me through a white mist. He was wearing his favourite jumper and looked completely healthy. Once he was close enough to speak, he told me he'd come to say goodbye. With that, he walked off into the mist again.

I woke up crying my heart out, convinced that he'd died. I had no evidence of course and he was the youngest and healthiest of my uncles. I kept telling myself I was being silly. Later that morning, I asked my mother to come and collect me since I felt too poorly to get the train. Before we began to gather up my luggage, she sat down on the sofa and said she needed to tell me something.

"I've got some bad news," she'd said. "I'm so sorry to tell you this, but your uncle passed away in the night from a heart attack. The doctors didn't know until it was too late. His GP had dismissed it as indigestion."

I had hoped that doing meditation was going to help but it didn't. It would do, and massively, later on, but at this early stage I'd been reading and listening to a lot of words about luminosity and peace without any understanding. I was still being tossed and turned on the river of life and now my little boat was smashing against rocks. We all want happiness and freedom from pain but this doesn't come naturally. It can take time and work and, when you're in the middle of grief, you just don't have that headspace.

I once came across a useful metaphor about this. Imagine life is like being in an aeroplane and, when things are going well, the 'plane flies smoothly. When bad things happen, we're temporarily thrown out of the 'plane into freefall with the ground coming towards us at an alarming rate. To prevent this, we need a parachute. Well, we can't make a parachute while hurtling toward the ground so we make it in times of relative peace and calm. When we have support and life is going a little bit more easily for us, then we have to find the time to get the fabric, learn how to make the pattern and start sewing. It takes time to make a good parachute. Then, if life throws us out of the aeroplane of comfort, we can open our parachute and glide down to the ground in safety. We are no longer smashed on the rocks of suffering every time something awful happens.

The trouble is, when we have times of relative calm we want to embrace that time and eat ice cream with our friends. Or maybe we just get busy with work or caring for relatives or doing projects. We don't think about the importance of the parachute in those times because we're not actually falling. The aeroplane is flying along perfectly well.

But if we don't create our parachute of mental and emotional resilience, whether that's by a faith of some kind, with meditation or other forms of mind training or emotional therapy, we'll be shocked when we next fall out of the 'plane. One of the awful truths about life is that bad things do happen. We all need parachutes.

Although I'd learned the art of relaxation and I had the benefit of my psychotherapy and occupational therapy training, I still found myself hurtling towards the ground with a parachute that had holes in it. I needed to look at that when things got better but, at this moment, I couldn't see that things would ever get better.

The day after my mother died, Matt drove me to the house. My brother was there, looking after my father and we all sat around in shock, talking to a Macmillan nurse. She said she would support my father as best she could since he was clearly going to struggle on his own. I grabbed a valium from my mother's medicine cupboard and cradled my cooling tea, wanting to believe my mother was in Heaven being cared for by kind celestial beings. I wanted to believe she was no longer suffering, that she was looking down on all of us. But I didn't believe it. All I knew for certain was that my mother wasn't on the Earth anymore and I would never hear her soft, contralto voice again.

During the funeral service, I couldn't sing a note. My father tried his best but, like my brother, was no singer and we stood like a row of mute birds on a wire, our hearts taut to breaking point. As I held my father's arm and gently walked him back up the aisle, he broke down and wept openly, his cries loud and uninhibited. I'd never see him like this before. He was normally calm and quiet, keeping his emotions to himself. I wanted to join him in the wailing but held myself together, needing to stay strong for him. I knew that if I let go we'd both end up in a heap on the cold flagstones.

English funerals can be like that, can't they? Rather controlled and well-behaved, all part of the British cultural reserve. We wear black, we cry quietly and we leave the grave when we're supposed to.

Some people in China employ people to help with the outpouring of grief so that the bereaved don't feel so alone. There's nothing worse than sobbing your guts up when no-one else is. Would it be better if we tore our clothes and writhed on the floor screaming until the grief naturally subsided? Would it result in us going down into a pit of depression and losing control? Or is it harmful to keep a lid on catastrophic emotions?

Outside, it was starting to snow. Tiny flakes filtered down from a bleak, white sky. By the grave, my aunt took my father's arm while an uncle held me to his side, exuding strength and comfort as the vicar began to speak. Once the coffin had been lowered, people produced single red roses, casting them lovingly into the grave. Then everyone looked at me with pale, stricken faces. I hadn't been told about this. I had no red rose.

Under a nearby bush, I saw a tiny white daisy, the sort you see in April. Somehow it had hung on throughout October and into November, not realising that summer was over. I bent down and picked it then walked to the graveside. Snowflakes drifted down, caressing the roses, and as I gave my last gift to my mother my heart broke.

As everyone left the churchyard, I rushed off to open up the house and then ran into the bathroom to have a really good cry until people arrived. Then I pulled myself together, blew my nose, washed my face and joined the wake. Everyone was rigid with shock, in tight control. I wanted to scream and claw at the wallpaper, but instead I poured drinks and smiled with a trembling chin at kind condolences.

When going through raw grief, stoical people try to get on with our day as best we can, even though we keep bursting into tears at the kitchen sink. Then, when the doorbell rings, we feel embarrassed that our eyes are red. But there's nothing to be ashamed of in grief. Our tears are a mark of our love, and if we don't cry it's often due to shock or feeling that we can't let go properly for some reason. We may want to reach out to others and have a hug and a cup of tea, but what others say isn't always helpful because they don't know how to respond or they come up with stock phrases.

At the time of my mother's death, I didn't want to be told that everything would be fine because everything was absolutely not fine. In fact, everything was terrible because death is dark and lonely and forever. Happily, I feel differently now and, although the pain is just as awful when I lose someone dear, knowing that there is something more – there is love, there is death and there is beyond – really helps.

When someone's grieving, perhaps we should ask them what they want rather than diving in, trying to make it 'better'. Something as simple as an apple pie or a card shows that we care. And when we say that we're going to be there for them, we should make sure we are. We should pay attention to them, giving our love and compassion, asking them what they need and trying to provide it. If we can't, maybe we can find someone else who can.

A few days later, I had an amazing experience. I was lying in bed alone, thinking of my childhood home and happy times, wide awake with eyes open. Thinking back to the funeral, an unexpected feeling of calm came over me and I felt my mother's presence. It was not a distinct form that I could see, but almost as if her essence was hovering in the form of a human-shaped cloud above me. Her mist filtered downwards and joined with me.

We became one and I could feel her within me, every cell of mine joined with every cell of hers. It was like being held as a baby, being in her womb and being both her and myself as adults all at the same time. She was me. I was her. I breathed. There were no words. After a few precious seconds she lifted away and I was myself again, alone.

"Please don't go just yet," I said.

She returned, then a few seconds later drifted away again. I felt thrilled to have had this experience, but even so my bleak beliefs about death remained and I couldn't stop myself from dismissing it all as imagination.

I was only allowed three days off work and then it was tough offering counselling to others when I could barely manage to breathe in and out. But my boss was supportive and, a few days later, friends from work said they would come round and support me in the evening. We had tea and cake in my cramped terraced house, huddled round the coal fire.

Timmy had been lying on my lap but when I started to cry she went out through the cat flap into the garden. Had my grief upset her? Of course not, I told myself, she'd just gone out for some fresh air. I didn't know then what I know now about animals' feelings. A few moments later, she came back into the room and deposited a dead mouse at my feet. I was quite taken aback and, for a moment, tears changed to laughter.

"It's a gift for you," said one of my friends as they picked the mouse up by the tail.

"Thank you, Timmy," I said.

My friend carried the mouse outside. A few minutes later, Timmy brought the mouse back in and dropped it at my feet again. We laughed. The mouse was removed. This happened repeatedly throughout the evening. I wondered if it was the same mouse.

"It must be," said my friend. "I keep lobbing it into the garden but she seems determined to give you a present. She's trying to cheer you up."

Our animals are so precious. Some of us are fortunate to have an animal that looks after us and knows when we're sad or in pain. Some animals are even so sensitive that they can pick up the scent of cancer and other forms of sickness in their owners. Others are less fortunate, with cats that stay aloof and expect us to serve them delicacies without so much as a word of thanks.

In the morning, I found out the sad truth. The garden was littered with corpses. Timmy rubbed against my legs, purring her morning greeting as I picked up each dead animal and laid them all in a row on the ground. There were thirteen altogether. My little darling had emptied the orchard of its mouse population in an attempt to ease my pain. I scooped her up and held her to my heart, thanking her profusely.

Up until that point, I had no idea that animals felt compassion.

FIVE

Spectral Visitors

When I grew up we'd always had a stunning garden and I learned the immense satisfaction of getting your hands in the soil and eating home grown vegetables. Having cleared my own garden of mouse corpses, I wondered whether perhaps trying to make the garden more beautiful might help me heal. I went to the nearby garden centre, a simple affair with no café or gift shop, just flowers and vegetables under polytunnels. There was a bare-rooted rose stalk in a plastic bag near the check-out. It looked dead.

"You can have that for a pound if you like," said the cashier.

"Really?"

"We were going to throw it out. You'll be lucky if you can get it to grow."

I thought for a moment about asking him to give it to me for free since they were going to throw it away but decided not to look a gift horse in the mouth. There was a small tag tied to the stem with an image of a pink flowering rose and its name.

Perpetua.

I liked the sound of that. Life was feeling fragile and temporary just now so to plant a rose that implied eternity felt right. I found a decent sized plant pot, covered the dry and shrivelled roots with soil and gave the rose a good long drink. I put the pot in a shady part of the garden and hoped for the best.

It can be a bit of a shock when we're young and find ourselves in the adult world. We discover that it can be a long, hard slog of getting up in the morning, going to work, coming home, cooking something and then doing it all again the next day. I was also looking after my father at weekends as well. He probably didn't have long and I wanted to make every day the best I possibly could. But I was getting tired.

Occasional trips to the Buddhist centre recharged me and I even went on a summer camp with Barbara, about fifty of us in a field in Bavaria. Beautiful vegan and vegetarian meals were served in the marquee three times a day and we enjoyed regular meditation sessions and talks. Lama Chime Rinpoche was there with some Tibetan monks although they were staying in a house attached to the camping area.

The monks spent all week creating a sand mandala. It was an intricate circular design – the kind you see in colouring books – but six feet in diameter and built up layer by layer out of fine, coloured sand into a bright, multicoloured, three-dimensional wonder. Each aspect of it was deeply symbolic and the detail was astonishing, taking hours and hours of painstaking work accompanied by the monks' chanting. Then, at the end of the week's final ceremony, they lifted the sides of the tent and let the winds of Bavaria blow the sand to the four directions.

Imagine making something in your craft room or workshop full-time for a week and feeling happy with the result. Then you have to break it up and scatter its parts far and wide. Could you do that? I know

I couldn't. Much of Buddhism is about letting go of attachments. This doesn't mean avoiding achievement, it's more about not identifying with things: "I did that, it's mine and I'm proud of it." I think many of us have a long way to go before we can truly learn this.

The sand mandala wasn't really about things that we make in our lives, though, like a painting or a career. It was about letting go of our false concept of the self so that, when our death comes, we suffer less. That was the bit that interested me.

Barbara is an adventurous, rebellious soul and it's a good job we weren't at school together because we would have got into so much trouble. One day, she and I took a cable car up the nearest mountain with a bottle of cheap Austrian wine and stood at the top shouting, "All is emptiness!" in Tibetan. Then a sudden storm arose and we had to shelter in a café.

When we got back to the camp we found that our tent had collapsed, destroyed by thunder and lightning. The ridgepole had been broken and our belongings were sitting in a puddle of water. Weirdly, ours was the only tent to be affected, but we tried not to take it personally. It was more than a little ironic that we'd been shouting about emptiness in Tibetan at the time. Maybe it was divine retribution for bunking off from our meditation studies. We were soaked through but kind people gave us fresh clothing and we dried our own things on the warm pipes in the toilet block.

Since this was the last night of our stay, the Rinpoche said we could have his room in the house and he would share with one of his Tibetan friends. In the morning, as we were cleaning our teeth, we could hear a strange noise that sounded like all the monks were chanting, "Phut, phut, phut," in soft voices.

Barbara told me that it's a practice called Powha, a meditation to make the moment of death easier for the self or for other people. Buddhist monks practise sending their consciousness out through the tops of their heads and into a spiritual realm of their choice. Many Tibetan Buddhists nowadays suggest using divine beings of other faiths in their instructions. For example, they encourage Christians to imagine God, the Holy Spirit or Jesus at the point of death. We may visualise any divine being of our choice in front of us and imagine being purified and healed by them, joining them in radiant light.

This makes esoteric practices more accessible for the rest of us. Powha can be done not just for ourself, but for someone we know who has died or even at the site of an accident. The idea is that, at the point of death, the person is guided 'to the light', through the presence of a divine figure.

When I was with Tony, we went on a six-month trip throughout Sri Lanka, India and Nepal. We discovered a temple displaying one of the Buddha's teeth and visited a monastery in Colombo where we chatted with monks about Psychology and Buddhism. If I hadn't been in love, I might have shaved my head at that point and put on saffron robes. The simple, quiet lifestyle with meditation and regular meals in a city on the coast seemed wonderful, but on reflection it might not have been that idyllic for a western woman alone in a very male world. Plus, I was very young and hadn't really started living yet so I'm glad I didn't.

We also visited Hindu temples in India and climbed up to the Swayambhunath temple in Nepal with its huge dome, or Stupa, at the top, decorated in all four directions by the all-seeing eye of Buddha. This amazing experience became even more dramatic when we were both attacked by monkeys who wanted our bread.

Later, I got the chance to travel with Matt. This trip was one I'd wanted to do for a while, having read the inspiring book *A Journey in Ladakh* by Andrew Harvey, a memoir describing travelling to this wonderful place and his life-changing experience of meeting a Tibetan Buddhist teacher. Five years after Andrew's visit, Matt and I also took the hair-raising bus journey from Kashmir to Ladakh.

One monastery we went to had a dimly lit corridor, its walls decorated with paintings of dancing skeletons. Beyond this was a tiny, hot and dark room in which loomed an enormous and terrifying, crumbling sculpture of what looked like a demon with many arms and legs, crushing skulls under its feet. It was made even creepier by having its face covered with an old tattered cloth.

All these scary images and the apparent intense focus on death made me wonder whether Tibetan Buddhism was right for me. Yes, I wanted to deal with my fear of death but not all day every day. I wanted comfort and hope, not skull-crushing demons and chanting and ritual. Some other aspects of the religion, like oracles and magic, also creeped me out. Even though my teacher Lama Chime Rinpoche had not asked me to do any of the rituals, I still felt that I needed something less intense so I decided to go back to the simple style of Hinayana meditation I'd learned at university. With this, you just focus on your breathing and practise feeling compassion.

There are many types of Buddhism. Hinayana is known as The Lesser Vehicle but it is not 'lesser than the others', it's just supposed to be a slower route to enlightenment. I wasn't in any hurry. I just wanted to calm my mind down.

Have you ever done a meditation on compassion? If you've looked at any mindfulness exercises, you'll have noticed that it's a key component. But it's not as easy as it looks.

One of the exercises is to focus on somebody you love, perhaps a pet, a relative or a friend. Feel the love for that person inside your heart and meditate on its warmth for a few moments. Then you let that person dissolve in your mind and bring your awareness to someone else, someone who is neutral such as a person you've met on the bus or in a shop. Now generate the same feelings of compassion for that person as you did for the person you love.

Here's the tricky part. Let that person's image dissolve and replace it with someone you dislike. Maybe you're having problems with a colleague at work or a neighbour. Imagine that person and wish them exactly the same level of compassion. This is always difficult but it can be possible with practice.

And what many people find most difficult is having to send that compassion to oneself. In our Western culture, we're taught not to be selfish and to think of the needs of others. But having self-compassion is not being selfish. In fact, without self-compassion it's hard to heal truly from life's hurts. I decided to practise this in the hope that I could overcome my awkwardness about being kind and forgiving to myself.

Before long, the Perpetua rose actually started to bloom and the various flowers I'd sown the previous autumn were thriving. Timmy enjoyed relaxing on my lap in the evenings and my job was going well. I'd been promoted and had completed the first year of a psychotherapy diploma. Although I looked to the outside world like I was coping, I was still regularly incapacitated by waves of grief and could feel myself slipping further and further down in mood. I was exhausted too and checked in with my GP to see if I was okay. As soon as I sat down in his office, I burst into tears. Having told him how I was feeling, he immediately signed me off for two months. I was to rest and recuperate from the combined overload of grief and work.

Many of us carry on when we should stop. We just don't see the warning signs and we think we're invincible. No-one is that strong.

A few weeks later, having had lots of relaxation and Timmy's care, I gained enough energy to visit my old housemate Kerry at a pub on the East Coast. It turned out to be a life-changing trip. Up to that point, I'd always snarled at people who say, "Everything happens for a reason." Well of course things happen for a reason, it's cause and effect and all that. Things fall to the ground due to gravity and some people have green eyes due to genetics. This doesn't mean that the apple was meant to land in that particular place or that the person was meant to have green eyes.

The trouble is, if we really believe that every single thing happens for a reason, then we risk making impulsive and potentially dangerous decisions. For example, we could choose to dive into a relationship because we feel it's come at such an amazing time, or we could choose to rent or buy a house because some coincidence has made us think it's meant to be. But that relationship or house might turn out to be a complete disaster. On the other hand, someone who believes there are no coincidences could then say that we were supposed to learn a lesson through that mistake. This just becomes a circular argument!

Yet, the series of coincidences that happened this particular evening almost had me believing in destiny.

If I hadn't been given time off, I wouldn't have been able to visit Kerry because I would have been looking after my father. In fact, I'd seen him earlier in the daytime to make sure he was okay before setting off. If I'd decided not to take this trip after all, I wouldn't have been in the right part of the country to hear the local radio advertisement that would rescue me from my doldrums. If we'd gone to the pub in Kerry's car, which was something we discussed earlier, we'd almost certainly have been chatting rather than listening to the radio. Then, on the way in my car, there was the storm. Due to this, I couldn't get the normal station I listen to so I'd switched the dial to the local one.

Later, I would come to understand that sometimes things fall into place rather miraculously and that not everything is 'a coincidence'.

The signal was distorted by interference but I managed to hear an advertisement asking for someone to go out to the South Seas, all expenses paid, for a film project sponsored by the BBC. I couldn't believe my ears. Sometimes, at our darkest moments, rays of light shine through. I got the job and it did prove to be a life-enhancing experience, the benefits of which I'm still reaping today. Perhaps most importantly, I was lifted out of my personal troubles and given a new focus. So, yes, sometimes it's good to pay attention to things that seem like outrageous coincidences.

When I returned from my adventure, I started working freelance in the community and at a local GP surgery. Being in charge of my own hours meant that I could earn enough to get by and still have time to look after my father without burning out. He seemed to be coping all right, with a home-help and meals-on-wheels, but tragically this was an illusion. In reality, he was desperate. One day, I got a shocking phone call from his home-help.

"Your father isn't well," she said. "He says he's taken too many Paracetamol."

My heart leapt. I had no idea whether this was deliberate or an accident, so I drove there as fast as I could, finding him in a terrible state. The not-so-helpful woman had left him on his own, staggering around the kitchen and crying. He said taking the pills had been intentional. It was clearly the act of a desperately sad man, brought to his knees by grief.

No child should ever have to face something like this. Our parents are supposed to be rock solid, aren't they, not fragile and human like us. However, everyone has their limit and even parents collapse some-times. They deserve our attention and care, and no-one should have to suffer alone. I was rigid with tension and sick with panic at the thought of the torment he must have been through, building up to this. And why hadn't he asked for help earlier? He knew I was a therapist. I was working in mental health at this point and I had all the right resources at my fingertips. But parents don't ask for help, do they, because they know they're supposed to be reliable.

I got him to tell me how many he'd taken then I called for help. He kept pacing up and down, with me supporting him physically every step because I didn't want him to fall asleep. He kept flitting in and out of reality, one moment aware of where he was and the next he'd be living in the past. At one point, he asked me where my mother was. Unsure what to say, I gently tried to remind him that she'd passed away – how can you do that gently? You can't. But I couldn't pretend either – and the news hit him like a sledgehammer, knocking his knees from under him, collapsing him into a heap of bones and old trousers.

I hugged him on the floor for a bit while he cried and then helped him to his feet, reassuring him that my brother and I would look after him and find him somewhere nice to live near me. It was quite clear that he couldn't carry on living alone. A few moments later he'd forgotten all about it again. All this time, I was simply trying to keep myself strong for him but it's so tragic to watch a parent struggle. And dementia is such a cruel beast, a dreadful disease. I came to realise that if he asked about my mother again the best thing to do would be to deflect the question, find out what he thought was happening and go with that. I wasn't his therapist, I was his daughter. It wasn't for me to help him come out of this; we needed to go through this together with professional support.

We found him a good care home a few miles from my house, where his health improved with good nursing care, counselling and better nutrition. We had to use the money from the sale of the house to pay for it all. His mood lifted and he seemed to forget completely that his dear wife had died. Indeed, for him, she was alive and well and he often commented that she was walking past or busy with something in another room. This seemed to keep him far less agitated, so I and the staff let it be.

Sadly, I didn't think for a moment that my mother was actually visiting him from beyond. At that time, I hadn't heard that our loved ones often do visit us. I just put it all down to my father's hallucinations protecting his sanity. I guess we all want to believe that those who have passed on are free from pain and that the afterlife is a wonderful place to be. We want to show them our love and share our news. Many people do continue to talk to their loved ones after they've gone, through a photograph or just by looking up at the sky, whether they believe in an afterlife or not.

I think my father was mentally living about twenty years in the past, in his happy time. Despite occasional episodes of agitation, he remained happy enough in the care home for the next year, where the staff were wonderful and looked after him well. Then, one day in early February, we'd been having a chat in his room when something very strange happened. He was on good form that day. Clear and lucid. Having chatted for a while about some of the other residents with his usual dry wit, he turned towards the door and smiled in greeting.

"Hello?" he said.

I turned to look but there was nobody there and the door was shut. I assumed he was seeing my mother again yet there was a look of surprise on his face that showed me that wasn't so. His polite tone implied this was someone he didn't know.

"What can you see?" I asked. He continued to smile a warm welcome into the empty space near the door.

"They've come to help me cross over," he said quietly.

I'd never heard him use that kind of spiritual language before. This was way out of my comfort zone.

"How does it feel to see them?" I asked, noticing my therapy language.

"It's quite nice really."

He smiled, still gazing at the door. I searched his face for signs of distress but his features simply held mild anticipation and welcome. After a few moments he told me they'd gone. I wondered whether they'd said anything else to him and what they'd looked like, but I didn't ask. I think I was scared to find out more so we chatted about other things until it was time for me to go. I gave him a kiss on the cheek, saying that I would see him again soon, and as I reached the door of his room and turned to him he held my gaze for a moment and smiled. I think we were both holding the other in memory, knowing that each visit could technically be the last.

Before I drove home, I mentioned what had happened to the nurse in charge. She said that 'visits from the other side' were very common as people approach death. My mind boggled. This woman, a capable and skilled nurse with years of experience working with the elderly and the dying, was talking in a completely pragmatic way about spiritual visitations.

I have since learned that hospice nurses regularly see their patients having deathbed visions and reaching out their arms as though taking the hand of someone just above them. They tell the nurses that they've seen their father or mother, or other people who passed away a long time ago. What's extremely reassuring to me, since I love animals so much, is that many people see their long-lost dogs, cats and even rabbits.

I guessed the end was close so I asked the nurse if he could have a vicar to deliver communion and she said she would organise it. The next day, I met the vicar at the home and told him a little about my father's recent history, although I missed out the bit about celestial visitors.

"I'll wait in the lounge," I said.

"Why don't you join us?"

"Oh, well... um, I'm not really a believer."

"That's fine." He paused, his eyes kind. "Be prepared. Most people only live a couple of days after having taken their final communion."

My heart began to thump but as usual I didn't show my feelings. I just nodded. Then when the service was over I went to my father's room. Having had a chat and a cup of tea, we said our usual farewell. I had such a strong feeling that this was our last goodbye and I had to force myself to walk down the corridor and out to my car.

The next morning, a phone call told me that he had died peacefully in his chair with a nurse by his side. He'd told the staff that he was looking forward to seeing my brother that day, then he'd passed away quietly with a gentle smile on his face. It was shocking to see him later, his face relaxed as though asleep. The staff left us alone for as long as I needed but eventually I knew I had to leave him. I hadn't been given this option with my mother, I was just handed a carrier bag with her dress, some slippers and her wedding ring. That was all.

My father hadn't taken a lot of possessions with him to the home. His winter duffel coat, new and hardly worn, was in the wardrobe so I slipped my arms into the sleeves and pulled it around me, enveloped by the thick, warm wool. The coat was way too big and felt comforting, like being hugged. Then as I turned to leave his room, I paused in the doorway to look back. I felt adrift, my childhood over. Death had taken both parents and it would take me too one day. A cold terror began to creep over me.

I put my hands in the pockets of the big, warm coat and felt something. A tube of Smarties. I'd given them to my father very recently and they hadn't been opened. When my brother and I were very young, our father would take us along a local footpath to some fields every Saturday with me in the pushchair and my brother trotting alongside. When we reached the first stile it would be time for what my father called a "sweetie stop". We'd usually have some Smarties before returning home. If I hadn't put on his coat, I wouldn't have found his final gift when I really needed it, our last sweetie stop.

I didn't feel safe to drive straight away. I sat in the car, looking at the care home, and felt a slight shift in my understanding. It had always been easy to dismiss any apparent spiritual events that were personal to me alone, but it was completely different when that experience came from someone else and was verified by others. In this case, it was my father who'd seen something, not me. And the nurse had said it was a common phenomenon. Was it possible that I'd been wrong all along and that he had occasionally seen my mother for real?

Even if you have no religious belief, the amount of evidence for deathbed visions is overwhelming.[4] Researchers have found that visions of deceased loved ones and pets appearing at people's bedsides at the hour of their death is extremely common and provides comfort to the dying. Interestingly, a lot of people were uncomfortable talking about this to their caregivers for fear of ridicule. Perhaps many of us have experiences that we don't share in case people think we're crazy. I now believe that we do see our loved ones, but at the time of my father's passing this was all brand new to me.

I remember Barbara telling me once that she had a ruptured pancreas when she was travelling in Thailand. She had the whole tunnel-towards-the-light experience and, just before she got to the light, Lama Chime Rinpoche appeared to her and told her that it wasn't her time yet.

I realised it was time for me to sit up and take note. There's scepticism, then there's pig-headed denial. I didn't want to go back to my old way of thinking because that's where my fear lay. My father had given me such wonderful gifts: a warm coat that felt like a hug and some sweets to remind me of our happy days. And the greatest gift of all was this new glimmer of hope that there may be a bigger picture to life and a spiritual world in which real beings care for us.

---

4   See *The Significance of End-of-Life Dreams and Visions* (P Grant et al, https://www.nursingtimes.net/clinical-archive/end-of-life-and-palliative-care/the-significance-of-end-of-life-dreams-and-visions-04-07-2014/)

SIX

Premonitions

A few months later I had to attend another funeral, for the mother of a neighbour who had, over the years, become a friend. I was offered a lift by friends of the family. However, for some weird reason I was plagued throughout the journey with the idea that we were going to crash. There was no basis for this – the driver was competent and seemed to have his emotions firmly under control, so why was I feeling like this? I just couldn't shake off the image of us meeting with disaster. It was the same sort of feeling I'd had when I was a teenager, but this time it was even stronger and it was specific.

When we get a vague feeling that 'something is going to happen' it's called a premonition whereas precognition, or prescience, is when we know a particular event is going to happen. When I was a teenager I had premonitions, the feeling that something bad was going to happen shortly before walking straight into the hostile arms of the local girl gang. However, in the car on the way to the funeral, I knew we were going to have a car crash and that it was going to be bad.

Precognition is different to clairvoyance, as I understand it. A clairvoyant experience is when we're able to see something as it happens, from a distance, whereas precognition is dealing with the future. I'd had clairvoyant dreams in my early twenties, able to see things that I should not possibly have been able to see. At the time, I locked these events away in my mind because they were too scary to explore. The implications were too enormous.

The first of these dreams was about my uncle who had died suddenly and the next was about a friend. I hadn't seen her in three years. In the dream, she was lying by the side of the road and as I went past she held my gaze, looking longingly into my eyes as though she needed help.

I woke from this dream feeling strangely shaken but thought no more about it. But, the following two nights, I had exactly the same dream. Her eyes looked at me imploringly, desperate for some kind of help. I contacted her parents to get her postal address and wrote her a letter, asking if she was okay. She wrote back by return post, saying that she'd had a motorbike accident and had been lying by the road, calling for help.

I was stunned when I read her letter. There was no way I could have known that my friend was at the roadside asking for help. Although part of me was quite excited about this experience, I didn't tell anyone else and tried not to think too hard about it. I now realise that some deeper part of me had registered the event and that this was undeniable evidence that our minds can reach out to each other.

I suspect that this kind of phenomenon is far more common than the scientific community believes. Even my mother, who was a staunch atheist, came downstairs one morning and instead of stopping to have breakfast went straight to the telephone. I asked what was going on and she told me that she was worried about her sister because she'd had a terrible dream about her; even my mother was prepared to accept that clairvoyant or telepathic dreams could be a reality. Nowadays we are more open to alternative ideas and surveys suggest that a majority of people report having such experiences.

Memories of my premonitions and dreams bothered me as I sat in the back seat of the car on the way to the funeral. I'd never experienced true prescience before but the conviction that we were all going to end up in a heap of tangled metal got stronger with every passing minute. This crash was going to be spectacular. Not just a little bump but possibly lethal. However, to my massive relief, we got to the church in one piece and the idea of the mythical car crash suddenly felt silly.

Once the funeral and wake were over, we set off for home and, as we joined the motorway, thoughts of mangled cars surfaced again. The passenger next to me said that the motorway was making her nervous and asked if we could take the scenic route. The driver agreed and took the next junction off the motorway, driving along the A-roads through the Peak District at a more sedate pace.

I tried to relax. Surely this was safer?

Along one stretch of road, there was a long, low, drystone wall to our left beyond which was a drop down to some fields about ten feet below. Sheep were grazing peacefully. The weather was good.

BLAM!

Everything happened in slow motion. I curled forward, protecting my face with my hands, and felt the seatbelt bite into my shoulder as the car jumped the pavement. Then came the whiplash when I slammed into the seat in front and jackknifed back again as the car came to a halt, crumpled against the wall. I clambered out onto the road, staggering as though emerging from an explosion yet feeling eerily calm, almost relieved that the dreaded crash had actually happened and that we were all still alive. The only pain I felt was from my thumb where it had been bent back against the seat in front.

The white van that had rammed into us tried to pull back from the wreckage as though to escape. It was clearly their fault, coming from a side road without stopping. I didn't think about my wellbeing as I grabbed onto the driver's door.

"Stay where you are!" I yelled, amazed at the intensity of my rage. "I'm calling the police. Don't you dare move an inch."

The driver froze.

I went with one of the women from the car to a nearby house to call the police and to tell Matt I would be late. I told him I was okay. When we returned to the crash site there was a community ambulance parked on the road. The paramedics looked at me with concern.

By now, I was feeling a little dazed. Have you ever wondered what kind of animal you might be? I think I'm part cat because cats tend to slink away and hide when they're hurt. I was quite prepared just to get in a taxi with the others and go home without even thinking about whether I was injured.

"We were just passing," said one of the paramedics. "I think you'd better come with us."

"But I feel fine," I said.

He shook his head and pointed to the ambulance.

"In you go. Now."

The boot of our car was open so I reached in to get my rucksack, packed in case I'd needed to stay the night, and slung it casually over my shoulder. A second paramedic leaped forward.

"No you don't! Put the rucksack down, you're in no fit state to carry anything."

I was the only one to get into the ambulance and I remember feeling puzzled about this as we drove away. After a few minutes we pulled over. Although I kept telling them that I just felt a bit lightheaded and sleepy, they said they were concerned and had called a fully equipped ambulance to meet us. Once in the emergency ambulance, a different paramedic kept eye contact with me and asked lots of questions about my life, my job and Timmy.

"Since you're an Occupational Therapist," he then said, "I expect you know why I'm asking you all these questions."

Then it hit me.

"You're keeping me conscious?"

"Exactly. So please try to stay awake."

They took me to a small hospital just north of the city, one without a proper A&E department, and the paramedic carried my rucksack while I tottered into a waiting room. A nurse took my blood pressure and asked me to read the sight chart on the wall. I couldn't even read the top letters. I was beginning to ache all over and I just wanted to lie down and sleep.

"Your blood pressure is low," she said. "I'll come back later and take it again. When it's back to normal, you can go home."

No X-rays, not even a physical examination of my back or neck. I sat there like a girl in school detention, wondering when the nurse was going to come back and when I'd be able to see properly. Something was very wrong with how I was being treated but my brain was addled and I couldn't work it out. I knew I shouldn't have been left sitting on a chair on my own.

If proper scans had been taken, maybe the life-limiting, painful disability that followed could have been prevented or at least lessened in severity. There's something about medical professionals that make most of us behave in a compliant manner. Even though I was trained in medicine myself, I suffered white coat syndrome just like everyone else. Even if we're brought up to be assertive, it can be hard to challenge someone in a white coat or dark blue uniform.

They sent me home eventually without any treatment even though I wasn't feeling any better. The comforting thought of curling up on the sofa with Timmy had become overwhelming so I didn't argue. In a very peculiar way, a little part of my brain was even congratulating itself on having known the future, having seen that a major life-changing event was going to happen. This was good evidence of something. Even if I'd been convinced about the crash before we set off, I couldn't possibly have used that as an excuse not to go. As it was, the prescient feeling only came upon me when I was in the car. That crash was going to happen no matter what.

Still, right now, life felt brutal. I'd had too many losses in recent years. When we have multiple losses like this, it's bound to be more complicated than dealing with just one episode of grief alone. Perhaps we can use the same kind of coping strategies, the parachutes, if we have them, but the whole process takes longer. We need to allow ourselves a lot more time and care to come through it.

At first, I had twitching muscles in my hand and numbness in my face and feet, which didn't make medical sense to me. I was treated by a physiotherapist for a disc prolapse in my neck but I continued to get worse. Then I saw a specialist who simply told me it was a musculoskeletal injury of my neck and back and that I should expect some pretty weird symptoms.

"Above all, don't panic," he said, not very helpfully.

When I was in that car coming back from the funeral, I hadn't been afraid of travelling and I'd trusted the driver implicitly. Yet I knew the crash was going to happen. It was the same when I got pregnant a few months later that same year. I just knew that something terrible was going to happen to me in childbirth. I'd always wanted children and had been told that my neck injury wouldn't be a problem.

Friends were happy for me, they touched my belly and brought their babies for me to play with. Life is often full of suffering, so it's wonderful when we see new life coming into the world. It's a time of great celebration for everyone. Birth really does conquer death. I was just very sad that my parents weren't around to witness my gradually expanding body.

However, at about thirteen weeks, I began to lose some blood so I went to the doctor and he organised a scan. I lay on my back with Matt by my side while the nurse searched around with the ultrasound on my abdomen. At this point in the TV shows, they show you the beating heart and the cute little form curled up inside you and you turn to your partner and share the first smile of true parenthood.

Not for us, though. She continued to search around, a frown gradually forming on her face.

"I'm so sorry," she said. "You have what's called a blighted ovum. It's where the egg and sperm haven't come together properly but you still form a placenta. You are pregnant but there's no baby."

She put the ultrasound away and wiped me with a paper towel. Matt and I looked at each other bleakly, neither of us able to take in the truth. After an operation to make sure the pregnancy was properly over, I still felt nauseous. The smell of my secondhand armchair made me want to gag. I still wanted custard yoghurts. I was round, still wearing my maternity trousers, but apparently empty.

I lay on my back on the sofa with Timmy curled up on my lap, watching television. That afternoon, Oprah Winfrey's show was on and she was talking about guardian angels to a live audience. A guest on the show shared how she was aware of her own personal angels looking after her in times of stress. The audience had sugar-sweet smiles on their faces, as though they too shared this wonderful experience.

Do we all have guardian angels? If so, where were mine?

At the time, I thought the idea of beings from the next level looking after us, or our parents guiding us from beyond, was all complete nonsense. I was envious of the people on the programme. It seemed like so many people had a full awareness of benevolent spirits guiding them. I so wanted it to be true but, to me, it was all just a fairy story. Wishful thinking.

A few days later, I began to bleed again. As I called an ambulance and lay on my back with my feet raised, the feeling that I wouldn't survive childbirth returned. Yet… I wasn't giving birth, not really. Maybe this was the event that was to take my life? The black hole that had taken my parents loomed in front of me. I was rigid with fear and beginning to shake, my heart racing, my mouth dry. I was petrified.

Paramedics arrived and rushed me to hospital with sirens blaring. Once at the emergency department, my trolley dashed down corridors and banged through double swing doors just like in the movies. The bright lights on the ceiling rushed past as doctors looked down at me and trotted alongside. Once on the ward, Matt sat by me while the pain got worse. I didn't know it was possible to lose so much blood and stay conscious. I was told that I was still pregnant and was examined for an ectopic pregnancy. They said they needed to operate but the theatres were all full because there'd been a pile-up on the motorway that evening. A doctor said that he was going to induce labour.

"Just a few cramping pains," he said as he gave me an injection.

Just a few cramping pains, my arse. The pain was excruciating and I didn't even have the comforting thought of a baby at the end of the agony. I'd learned all the labour breathing techniques from the baby books but it was so sad to use them in this situation.

Fortunately, my mother had once given me some great advice while she was going through her treatment for cancer. She'd said that when life kicks you in the teeth, you have to take things one hour at a time. Then if things get really bad, focus only on the next minute in front of you. Then she'd looked me in the eye. "When things get impossible, take it one breath at a time." I held my mother in my mind and took one breath at a time.

Finally, there was a space for me in the operating theatre. By now, my body was shaking uncontrollably but I didn't want Matt to see how terrified I was so, as I was wheeled away at speed, I managed to give him a smile and a thumbs up gesture.

"It's just your nerves," said a nurse when I asked why I was shaking so badly. I didn't know whether she meant my physiological nerves or my emotional ones. My brain was certainly turning to mush as my muscles shook and the trolley dashed along the corridor.

'This is going to be fine,' I said to myself, 'as long as they transfer me from the trolley to the bed smoothly.' We should never make bargains like that. Of course they fumbled the transfer, banging my trolley against the table and jolting me. I heard a nurse curse mildly under her breath then just had time to think 'Oh s...' before I sank into the darkness I so deeply feared.

I came round utterly spaced out but relieved still to be alive. Then the next day I went into shock and nurses and doctors were rushing around me again, filling me full of IV fluids and lifting the end of the bed up. Modern medicine pulled me through and after five days I went home.

I'd never heard of a blighted ovum before and had no idea that, if not successfully treated the first time, it could become a life-threatening problem. At least my fears, my prescience, hadn't been literally true. I was still alive. Although if this that happened to me in my parents' era, or if I'd lived further from the hospital, I would certainly have died.

Once I'd recovered from the initial shock, I grieved my lost pregnancy for a long time. How many losses can one person take? I don't want to scare anyone with medical facts, but there is scientific evidence that multiple episodes of grief can lead to cardiac issues and other health problems. I knew this at the time, but what could I do?

It's hard to know where to start with the healing process. Yes, sometimes we just have to take things an hour at a time or even one breath at a time. Looking at all the losses at once just makes things worse so sometimes all we can do is look at what we need for today. Do we need a friend to talk to, a walk in nature or a good howl somewhere private?

Multiple losses can shake our confidence in the world and in ourselves. Each loss can compound the others. Grief is persistent. Even if our losses are years apart, we still tend to remember previous times and they can add together. It's normal for this kind of experience to lead us to feeling anxious or depressed. Sometimes we even blame ourselves for what has happened and our self-esteem plummets: we could have done better, been there more often, kept in touch.

It's so important to take care of ourselves and to ask for help.

I didn't know many people where we lived and was heavily reliant on Matt, which must have been a strain on him. My brother was kind too but there was little he could do as he lived far away. I now understand the benefit of staying physically near family. When we used to live in little villages, help in these tough times would have been readily available.

By now, my neck injury was giving me stronger involuntary movements and stabbing nerve pain in my hands, face and eyes. I couldn't sit in the pub with friends or go to a restaurant because the unsupportive chairs caused too much pain. I couldn't walk far or swim anymore. I was beginning to get scared. The doctors were unable to offer me any help.

Since driving was becoming too difficult, we decided to move to a house just down the road from the adult education centre where I worked part-time. The place Matt and I chose was a dilapidated, four-storey Victorian terraced house with ornate plasterwork around the ceiling and Minton tiles in the hallway. The kitchen was huge and there was a cellar and an attic. There was plenty of room for potential children in the near future, assuming we were luckier next time. Despite my awful experience and the current level and unpredictability of my pain, I still hoped for a family one day and the hospital had said there was nothing to stop me trying again for a baby.

A pleasant man took us on a tour of the house, showing us the small town garden and the original sash windows. When he opened the door to the attic, I couldn't suppress a gasp. On the wall opposite someone had painted, in huge black letters, the words, "You're all gonna die!"

"This is my teenage daughter's room," said the man, with a slightly embarrassed smirk.

Despite this message of doom, we decided to go ahead and put in an offer on the house. One of the first things I did in the garden was to ask Matt to help me plant the Perpetua rose. By now it had at least three branches and was producing a flurry of pink flowers. The scent was beautiful.

After her two-week indoor period, Timmy began to explore the garden. She seemed keen that there was an apple tree beyond the back wall. It probably reminded her of the orchard at the back of the previous house. She had somewhere to hunt and climb and a warm patio to lie on.

Luckily, we again had nice neighbours. On one side was a woman called Jo who had pets. A summerhouse stood against the back wall of her garden and, leaning against the kitchen wall, was a wooden sunflower picture. She told me it had been painted by her father and was designed to be left outside to cheer up the garden. Jo had a timid lurcher called Freya and two rescue cats, a tabby called Tabatha and a long-haired tortoiseshell called Dolly. Jo told me how she had adopted both cats from a rescue centre.

"Dolly was found in a taped-up cardboard box by the side of the canal. When she was found, she was in a terrible mess and her kittens were dead."

"That's so cruel."

"Dolly won't let anyone touch her except my youngest daughter and she won't come indoors. I put up that little summerhouse so she's got a nice warm place to live." I could see a round, fluffy cat sitting on a cushion. She looked comfortable but it seemed so sad that she was too afraid to come indoors.

"What will happen in winter?"

"I don't know," said Jo. "I just hope she's more trusting by then."

I had no idea at the time that Dolly would end up living with me and that she, like Timmy, would play a huge part in my spiritual journey.

Many years before, I'd had an astrological birth chart reading. Apparently, I was to have an active and interesting life right up until the age of thirty-six, and then there was a huge gap with only one further symbol on the page, many years later. I remember asking whether that meant I was going to die at that age. The man doing the reading paused, his face serious. For the first time in our session, I felt a flicker of fear in my belly. This man absolutely believed in what he was doing.

"Not necessarily," he said. "It's all a matter of potential."

Not necessarily?

He took a sheet of acetate with other markings on it and laid it over the top of the initial chart.

"So much depends on the choices you make. The first reading is one possible pathway. This is another. You may well live beyond thirty-six, but something will happen that will mean you have to spend the rest of your life in a radically different way and you'll spend your time processing the earlier part of your life."

Well, my thirty-sixth birthday came and went and, a few weeks later when nothing had happened, I let go of the idea of the birth chart. I was still suffering the consequences of the car crash but was making some slow progress. Then I awoke one morning and stretched. Pain shot through me and my neck made a disgusting squelchy sound. I could barely move.

The GP told me that I'd slipped a disc in my neck and would have to wear a neck brace. I had to give up work completely and went on sickness benefit. It hurt to wash my hair. I couldn't stand at the sink for more than two minutes or chop vegetables. My hobbies were over. I used to love playing the flute but that was now impossible, and I used to love art but it hurt to lift a paintbrush.

My old life seemed to be over.

My parents were dead, I'd lost my job and my identity as a therapist, my hobbies were too painful and I'd lost a pregnancy. It's so easy to slip over the cliff of despair when times hit us hard. In fact, there was a period of time where I realised I was even fantasising about suicide. For a while, I didn't tell anyone because I knew this was only a cry for help.

I tried, instead, to think of all the things I actually could do without pain. There wasn't much. I could still speak and I could still think. I still had Timmy by my side, purring gently. Somewhere deep inside, I probably still had my sense of humour and I certainly had my imagination. Speaking, thinking and imagining.

Maybe I could be a writer?

I mentioned to my brother on the phone that I wanted to try and write about my travel adventures, to keep myself sane, so he bought me a voice-activated Dictaphone. It was a fantastic piece of kit. I would lie down by the fire and repeat a sentence over and over, playing it back until I was happy with it, then roll onto my side and write it in my notebook. I would then roll onto my back again and start the next sentence.

After a few weeks of rest, I was strong enough to sit up and use my father's old typewriter, one sentence at a time. It took me a week to write a page, which was frustratingly slow, but it also gave me something to wake up for. It gave me a purpose.

I gradually improved enough to be able to walk a little but it was clear that I couldn't return to work. I remembered the birth chart. Well, I hadn't died, which was something to be glad about, but I could see that life was going to be different from now on. Was this disability

79

'meant to happen' and if so why? Fate seemed rather cruel, which is why I still rejected the notion that I was for whatever reason meant to live a life of pain. If there's any truth in astrology, how much free will do we have? Rather than one single path, do we have a series of predestined possible routes through life, each leading to a different destination depending on our decisions?

I got in touch with a physical therapist, who helped me get back on my feet in a way, and went to my GP to arrange counselling. However, I wasn't too impressed with the level of care so I used my meagre savings to pay for a private therapist. This wonderful woman pulled me out of the pit of despair and, over time, enabled me to heal emotionally.

SEVEN

Soul Families

The next autumn, I received a letter from my cousin telling me that my dear auntie, the one I used to spend summers with as a child, had passed away unexpectedly in her sleep. The news tore at my heart. I couldn't travel to the funeral because I could only manage a couple of minutes in a car, so I decided to hold a ceremony of my own.

I was, by this point, able to walk the few yards to the top of the nearby park and sit on a bench under the trees. I tried to be grateful for the improvement I'd made, but was frustrated that my progress was slow and my life was still so limited by pain. The day of her funeral was a good day for me physically, so I went to the top of the park and found a secluded place among the trees. I took a jam jar of flowers, a candle and some matches, a pad of paper and some pens. I didn't really know what I was doing but it felt right somehow.

Every culture has its own death rituals. We need them because, when we get the shocking news that someone has died, we often don't know what to do with ourselves. The world no longer seems to make sense. We come together in families and groups to mourn, share happy memories and celebrate the life of the person who has just gone. These rituals give us a sense of meaning and continuity and, for that brief time, we feel in connection with the deceased. If we happen to be alone at this point, then making up our own ritual is all we can do.

The flowers were for my aunt because she loved wildflowers and had taught me all their names; the pen and paper were to write a poem for her and the candle and matches were to send my message on its way. If I'd been a complete believer in such things this might have been understandable behaviour, but for me it was extraordinary. I'd never done anything like this before.

Even though I was fairly well hidden, I still felt nervous about someone seeing me sitting like a pixie at the base of the silver birch trees. It was a sunny autumn day and the grass was soft. I pictured my dear cousins at the church and hoped they didn't mind me not being there. It's hard to explain to people that you live with severe chronic pain when you look normal.

I put the flowers on the grass and lit the candle. Memories of happy days with my cousins on the south coast flooded my mind: picnics on chalky clifftops with blue butterflies flitting across the sheep-cropped grass, sunny days on the beach and happy, noisy Christmas holidays. I wrote a poem telling my aunt how much I loved her and, just before I predicted the service would be over, I burned the page. I had the instinctive, whimsical notion that my words might reach her that way.

To my great surprise, a gentle breeze, a zephyr, sprang up from the south, travelling towards me like an invisible comet. It paused and the air around me got brighter, lighter, as though the sun had come out a second time. I sensed the presence of something powerful all around me and I was stunned. Could it be my aunt?

"If this is you," I whispered, my voice trembling with hope and confusion, "then, thank you."

I still didn't believe in a Holy Spirit looking after us in our hour of need or a kind old man in the sky yet here I was, whispering to the trees with my eyes out on stalks at the brilliance of the light, hoping to believe even if just for a moment. My previously closed mind seemed to be opening a crack.

A few heartbeats later, the light dimmed back to normal sunlight and the breeze began again. This time, there was a sense of something travelling away from me. Had all the love, kindness and joy contained in my aunt been set free on the wind? Had she paused by me to say goodbye before whooshing off to Heaven? Or maybe I was going completely barking mad with accumulated loss. Feeling a little wobbly, I packed up my things, got back home and didn't say a word.

Matt and I had been together for ten years so it was a great delight to me when he proposed marriage. The wedding itself went well, although I must admit I floated through it on a haze of painkillers while wearing a full plastic neck brace. My new GP had given me the medication and had sent me to the local Occupational Therapy department where they made the brace for me. It provided a lot of relief although it was rather hot and bulky. I lay flat right up until the car came to collect me and then lay flat again after the reception. We had no party in the evening as I knew I wouldn't have been able to tolerate it. Despite this, it was a gentle, romantic day.

Shortly afterwards, I got the results of the laparoscopy I'd had earlier in the year. They told me I had damaged fallopian tubes and only a two per cent chance of conceiving a child. I wondered yet again how much free will we have in life and how much is meant to be.

The problem is… people often say that things happen for a reason when happy events occur, for example somebody meets a new partner, gets a good job in unlikely circumstances or moves to a better area having lost their home. You don't tend to hear anybody saying that the atrocities of war or childhood cancer are meant to be. To do so implies a rather cruel divine plan in which we are simply pawns. I had so wanted a baby. The pain of my grief was raw.

I wondered whether a puppy would help. Timmy was now eleven years old, having grown into a sleek and healthy middle-aged cat with a beautiful, relaxed temperament. I loved her dearly. She lay by my side a lot of the time and across my feet or between my ankles at night. How would it change things if I got her a canine brother or sister? How hard was toilet training? How would I manage with my pain? All these were sensible thoughts but my main concern was for Timmy, that she would accept the new situation and play nicely.

I went on the RSPCA waiting list as a prospective 'dog parent', had the house and garden vetted and then it was just a question of time. Finally the call came telling me that a litter of puppies were looking for owners.

When Matt and I arrived at the shelter we found at least ten people crowding around the wire-fenced enclosure. Six puppies and ten people. This didn't look good. We jostled at the fence, trying to get a good position. I could hear all the other neglected, abandoned adult dogs in their pens shouting, "Don't bother with the puppies! Pick me. Over here. Pick me!" I knew that if I went over to see them, I'd gather each and every skinny, sad dog in my arms and cry into their fur as I hustled them all into the car. So I stayed where I was, breathing a silent apology.

A ripple of excitement ran through everyone as one of the staff went round the back of the pen. She smiled at us.

"Are you ready?"

"Yes," we all said in unison. We'd been told to stay quiet and calm so as not to scare the pups but as soon as the litter of round, soft bodies emerged from the sleeping area, we all began to "Oooh" and "Aaah" and call them.

Each one was a darling. I was flooded with the absolute certainty that one of these was meant to be mine. They skidded on the washed concrete of their pen, rolling over each other in play. Four looked like tiny golden Labradors, one was sable, like a tiny Alsatian, and the only boy of the group was black and white like a Collie. They all had cute, oversized paws and floppy ears and didn't seem in the least bit fazed by all the commotion.

The humans tried to push each other out of the way like people do at the start of a department store sale.

Fabulous puppies. For today only. Buy now.

I was spellbound. I knelt down and placed my fingers through the links in the wire fence as Matt stood back, observing. The sounds of the people chattering and cooing faded in my ears as a golden female came up to me. She was the smallest of the group and seemed timid. Her eyes met mine in a connection that went soul-deep.

Have you ever met someone you felt you've known forever? The instant you meet them, there's a strange kind of recognition. They feel almost like family even though you've never seen them before.

"Hello," I murmured.

Three of the other puppies had now noticed the people and were coming forward, bottoms wriggling in delight. The sable and the black and white one continued to play fight, nibbling each other's ears and skidding around. The golden puppy lifted one paw and touched my fingers. I'd been chosen.

"This one," I said to Matt. "She's the one."

Matt was hesitant. He pointed out that she looked timid whereas the sable one seemed more confident and might be easier for us to handle as first-time dog owners. He was probably right. He was thinking sensibly, unlike me.

At that moment, the sable one seemed to notice me for the first time, came over to her sister and lifted a paw to touch my hand. The connection was immediate and just as strong as with the other puppy. It was as though I'd known both of them forever and the three of us were supposed to be together for the rest of our lives.

There's an idea in the spiritual community that sometimes souls incarnate together in the same lifetime because they're part of a spiritual family. We know it because we can feel it. We connect deeply, immediately, without knowing why and feel like we've known one another before. These people often turn up in our lives when we need guidance the most and whenever we're with them we feel uplifted and energised.

This isn't a simple matter of friends who share the same interests and who make us laugh and feel good. This goes way deeper; some people may only meet one person like this in their lifetime whilst others meet more. We call them our soulmates or soul family. They don't even have to be human. I felt this way about both these puppies so could I have both? My neck was beginning to ache despite the support of the brace. At that moment, the RSPCA worker came over with a clipboard.

"Has anyone decided yet?"

It would have been foolish to take both so I had to decide. The darker puppy began chewing my hand and my heart melted. This was impossible. Matt repeated that the sable one was confident, in the middle of the pack, not like the golden one who looked nervous. But I was in love. With both.

If I'd been able-bodied, I would definitely have wanted to take both. But I couldn't make this decision with my heart, it had to be with rational, health-based dog logic. A nervous dog might have been too much for my frail body. However, to this day, I regret letting the golden one slip through my fingers.

I could feel the sable puppy's soft tongue on my fingers and I knew that I was prepared to fight for her, even die for her, despite the fact that I could hardly stand up. We filled out the paperwork and I waited for what felt like an eternity with my mind in a whirl. Everything was going to change. I was going to be responsible for a tiny being. My tummy flipped with excitement. Finally my puppy was placed in my arms and I kissed the top of her head and nuzzled her, breathing in her scent, a comforting mixture of damp autumn leaves and wolf.

Anyone who's ever cared for a young animal has probably sniffed them manically. It's intoxicating. Have you ever stood in the kitchen and just sniffed and sniffed, not able to get enough of that heart-warming scent? And we don't even care if someone comments on our behaviour because we're in love and that's that.

The RSPCA worker pointed to the collar round my neck.

"Are you going to be all right?" she said. "Puppies are hard work."

"Of course. I'll be fine," I said, giving her my brightest smile. Matt drove home while I held the puppy on my lap. She seemed completely unafraid and enjoyed looking out of the window as the world flew past.

Timmy was sitting on the stairs when we got home so I held the baby dog in my arms and introduced them to each other.

"This is your new sister," I said. "She doesn't have a name yet." Timmy shot me a withering glance and retreated upstairs to the bed-room with a flick of her tail. "I still love you," I called after her. "You're still the best cat in all time and space."

I plopped my puppy's huge paws onto the Minton tiled hallway and watching her gallop into the kitchen, wagging her pencil-thin tail at her exciting new world. I decided to call her Betty.

"Welcome home, little dog."

My puppy book recommended putting a ticking clock, wrapped in a blanket, in the animal's basket for the first few nights to provide a comforting heartbeat sound. Betty didn't look as though she needed comforting heartbeat sounds but I didn't want to take the risk. Then, once the excitement of the first day was over, she may feel a bit weird. She'd been snuggled up with her brothers and sisters for the past eight weeks and was now going to be all alone in a strange house for the first time.

To prevent her from bothering Timmy, Matt put a child's safety gate at the foot of the stairs. It wouldn't stop Timmy because she could slip through the bars, but it would provide a temporary barrier for puppies. Once Betty was settled, I went upstairs to see Timmy. She was on the bed, half asleep, and she lazily opened one eye when I approached,

"Your new sister is called Betty," I said, stroking her soft ginger head. Timmy was the most beautiful cat in the world and so gentle in nature. She never scratched or bit. She was brave, kind and friendly. "You know I love you with all my heart." She purred and rolled onto her back. "So I hope you'll come downstairs soon and meet her," I crooned. "And you'll be the best of friends one day. Would you like some supper?"

She ate her food with her usual enthusiasm. Clearly, the sounds of the squeaking toys coming from downstairs hadn't put her off.

That first night, I felt a little anxious about leaving Betty alone but she slept through the whole night without crying. I felt proud of her. After feeding Timmy the next morning, I went downstairs to see her. When I opened the kitchen door, she jumped out of her bed to greet me, her tiny tail wagging in circles. Life felt good again.

One of the beauties of having a puppy if you're childless is that you can join in motherly conversations with your friends, saying things like, "Yes, Betty does that too," and telling them about your puppy going to the toilet outside for the first time or going to a puppy party. Well, it isn't completely the same, but it helps. And sure enough, by the end of that first year Timmy and Betty had become inseparable friends. Betty acted like a mother, nudging Timmy along towards her food bowl at teatime and allowing her to share her bed when it was time to snooze. I had two of the kindest, friendliest pets in the universe.

I still had a lot of chronic pain and was too incapacitated to go back to work. My brother paid for me to see a back specialist who took X-rays and pointed out that my spine had been broken when I'd had that catastrophic fall from Tommy's back all those years before. I then saw a chiropractor who pointed out that my neck had also suffered impact damage where the skull meets the spine. The car crash had just made things a lot worse.

The jigsaw was gradually being pieced together. I was grateful for this professional help even though no-one was able to fix me like a mechanic might fix a car. With regular muscle therapy and careful pacing of activity, I shifted from desperation to acceptance. This didn't mean that I gave up hope but at least I knew there was a mechanical reason for my problems. It wasn't all in my head as I'd sometimes feared.

During this time, my marriage ran into difficulty. Despite a lot of effort to mend things, we ended up amicably agreeing to part company and I was able to keep custody of both Betty and Timmy. Despite the sadness, this led to one of those special moments when things seem to come together just as they should. If we pay attention to those moments, we can grasp new opportunities. Getting my first house as a single person was one of those moments.

I came across a cheap terraced house for sale in a rough area of town. I needed an affordable place as soon as possible so I thought it was worth a look. It was late summer and through the open doors I could hear the estate agent talking to other prospective buyers, his voice echoing in the empty rooms. I was upstairs, gazing vaguely out of the window at the paved and empty garden and wrinkling my nose at the smell of urine wafting from the bathroom. I'd been told that the previous owners had a disabled son who'd repeatedly urinated near the toilet, not in it. The whole place needed decorating and the sash windows didn't open.

It didn't seem promising. I was feeling delicate. How was I going to look after the animals on my own? Would I ever find love again? My future looked like a white fog and I couldn't see through it.

The neighbour's garden was paved and had pots of flowers along the walls. Two cats sat outside the back door, sunning themselves. That's when I noticed the artwork, a massive block of wood painted with bright sunflowers. I stared harder. How was this possible? It looked exactly the same as the one in my previous neighbour's garden. I made my way down the steep, narrow stairs and went next door.

"Sorry to bother you," I said to the woman who answered.

She seemed relaxed and welcoming. I felt my shoulders dropping a little.

"Yes?" she said, tipping her head slightly to one side.

Beyond her was a clean and compact living room with a sofa, a Victorian fireplace and stripped wooden floors. I got an impression of how these houses could look if they were given proper care.

"I'm just wondering what it's like around here," I said. "I'm looking at buying the house next door." I wanted to get on to talking about the artwork in the garden but felt awkward.

"It's fine," she said. "We've never had any trouble."

At that moment, a Collie dog ran through from the kitchen, barged through her legs and sniffed at my hands. I patted his head.

"This is Bryn. I'm Laura."

"Hi, I'm Helen," I said. "I've got a dog called Betty."

"Ah, that's nice. There's a park at the end of the street and not far away is the big park. There's a café there. I meet my Mum and sister every weekend with our dogs." This was my cue.

"I love that park. I'm only moving from nearby." I paused. "Can I ask you a strange question?"

"Of course."

"I'm just wondering about the artwork, the sunflowers, in your garden. My neighbour has a very similar piece."

"Really? That was painted by my father."

"Do you have a sister called Jo with a dog called Freya and cats called Tabatha and Dolly?"

"Yes!" Her eyes opened wide.

"Oh, my goodness! You'll never believe this. I've been living next door to her for years."

The house was in a cheap area popular with university students and had only been on the market a few days. I'd felt so alone and adrift just half an hour earlier, yet now I'd been given an anchor. I mean, what were the chances of finding a house next door to the sister of my old neighbour? I knew it was just a coincidence but it felt almost magical. I felt protected and guided somehow.

Breathing a huge sigh of relief, Betty, Timmy and I settled into our new home and enjoyed regular trips to the park with our neighbours, both new and old. I think Betty enjoyed the feeling of continuity as much as I did and Timmy loved basking in the paved garden. The only downside was that the neighbourhood was quite run down with a lot of broken glass and graffiti. Betty and I had to negotiate the pavement with great care and I kept an eye out for the gangs of youths, making sure no harm came to my best friend.

As autumn turned to winter, Timmy's hips became stiffer. Although she had tablets from the vet, she still suffered when the weather was bad. She kept trying to get on the sofa, putting her little white paws on the edge so that she could sit next to me, but wasn't able to jump up easily. Even though she wasn't showing any signs of distress, I decided to pop round next door for advice.

Laura said she could give Timmy some Reiki to make her more comfortable. Reiki held the same place in my mind as spiritual healing, a lovely idea but utterly unreal. Despite my misgivings, I politely agreed. She came round and sat close enough to touch Timmy.

"I have to ask her first," she said. "You can't force Reiki on anyone."

I nodded, trying to look suitably cooperative. The idea of telepathically talking to a cat seemed laughable but I didn't let my thoughts show. It's not always polite to tell people what we really think. If I had done so that day, Laura might have gone away and then I would never have learned what I came to learn later.

I guess Laura knew that Timmy was agreeing to healing because she leaned forward and cupped her hands near Timmy's shoulders. She was very gentle in her movements, her eyes partially closed as she slowly moved around, never actually making contact. Timmy's head, back, shoulders, hips and tail all got the same hand warmth from a few inches away. Timmy lapped it up as though she was being stroked.

Finally, Laura sat back.

"There. Let's see how she is. They often drink some water afterwards and then sleep." I was quite surprised when Timmy immediately got up and drank from the water bowl near the fire. I hardly ever saw her drinking indoors. She preferred rainwater. "That's a good sign," said Laura.

Then Timmy blew my mind by leaping up onto the sofa as if she'd never had any hip pain in her life. Could it have been the warmth from Laura's hands? Or had Timmy simply rested enough and now felt okay? Surely it couldn't be… spiritual.

"How?" I managed to say.

"It's healing energy."

"But how?"

She laughed good-naturedly at my confusion. "This is what I do at the weekends. I drive to the local animal sanctuary and give Reiki to any animal that's distressed or in pain."

"So, it really works?"

"Yes. It really works."

EIGHT

The White Whisker

Two weeks later, Timmy seemed sore again, so I popped round next door. I knew that if Reiki worked a second time, I really would have to re-evaluate my attitude. Laura came round and, within a few minutes, Timmy was once more absolutely fine just as before. This time she didn't drink the water but jumped up onto the sofa straightaway for a cuddle, sitting in her normal place to my right. It was her favourite spot when she wasn't sharing Betty's bed or lying between my feet at night.

"You know, I was seriously sceptical about this the first time," I said. "But now that I've seen it happen twice…"

Laura smiled in the way someone might if they were to show you how delicious chocolate was for the first time.

"You can train to do this yourself," she said. "I can give you the name of my teacher. It costs a little bit but then, once you've trained, you'll be able to treat Timmy whenever you want. And Betty too, if she accepts it."

"Really? Me?"

"Yes, you. I think you'd be really good at it."

Laura gave me the number of the Reiki teacher and also recommended a local massage therapist to help my poorly muscles. I thought
it was worth trying, even though money was now a serious issue.

As soon as I saw the masseuse's beautiful pine shed at the bottom
of her garden, I felt myself beginning to relax. It was clean and bright,
smelling of some unidentified essential oil. Outside the shed, a willow
tree swayed in the breeze. Gentle New Age music played. I lay on the
massage table and listened to the sound of a miniature water fountain
on a shelf nearby, trying not to think about wanting to wee. She started
off with a facial and, while I waited for the cucumber slices to soothe
my eyes, asked if I would like to receive some Reiki. Well, it seemed
to work for Timmy.

Life regularly offers us turning points and this was one of them. I
closed my eyes and sensed her moving her arms around near my head.
I could feel the warmth of her hands near me, a pleasant and relaxing
sensation. Then heat, I mean really strong heat like from an electric
fire, coursed down my body from my head to my toes. This wasn't just
the heat from her hands, this was something else.

Slowly and gently, she moved around my body, hovering her hands
over me. I felt like I was attached to some kind of battery charger. It
reminded me of the time I first discovered T'ai Chi Ch'uan in the early
Eighties. I'd always had a warring attitude between my scepticism of all
things other-worldly on the one hand and my ability to perceive chi on
the other. While I was 'standing firm like a mountain' or 'yielding like
fog', I would often sense the life force or chi running through me and
through other people. In fact, when I was doing my hospital training, I
got a reputation for easing people's headaches and common colds using
a mixture of chi and the knowledge I gained doing a Reflexology course.
These things didn't seem paranormal to me. The energy around people
just seemed a part of their body, so it didn't challenge my scepticism.
Isn't it ingenious how our minds can explain things away?

I went back to the lovely little hut in the kind woman's garden regularly after that and the Reiki I received helped me deal with my muscle pain. It also helped me decide to do the training myself.

Reiki comes from Japan and is an ancient healing technique. Rei means higher power and ki means life force, referred to as chi in China and prana in India. It means that a Reiki practitioner will enable the flow of universal life force through you. According to the International Centre for Reiki Training, anyone can learn to do this. It doesn't matter how 'spiritually developed' you are and you don't have to have any religious beliefs for it to work. And the wonderful thing is that it works on animals too – the Reiki teacher Laura had recommended specialised in working with animals and had an energetic German Shepherd who was a regular recipient of the energy.

My scientific brain kept rolling its eyes and telling me that this was all completely bonkers, while the part of me that wanted to help Timmy and wanted to be open-minded told the sceptical part of me to shut up. A true scientist doesn't ignore evidence or dismiss ideas without testing them.

Having done my training, I soon got the opportunity to try it out. Timmy was looking sore so I sat down by Betty's bed and quietened my mind. I placed my hands near Timmy's back and began to follow the instructions I'd been taught. To my delight, it worked and she seemed to love it. I could feel a definite connection flowing between us. When I'd finished, she stretched and jumped on the sofa like a kitten. I knew it couldn't be placebo or just the warmth of my hands. My closed-off mind creaked open another bit.

Another Christmas came and went. I was still very bothered by nerve and muscle pain so my GP sent me to a pain clinic at the hospital, where I was diagnosed with Myofascial Pain Disorder and Fibromyalgia. Basically, this meant that my muscles and connective tissue, if overused, were now prone to contracting and locking which then squeezed the nerves in my body and caused pain. 'Overuse' meant things like standing to wash up for more than five minutes or walking more than a few hundred yards. It is a disorder that often happens after trauma. I was given a course of physiotherapy, which helped a bit, but I still couldn't get back to work. It was enough just looking after myself and my animals.

In springtime, I decided to organise a birthday party for Timmy who was by now the ripe old age of twenty. I invited both Laura and Jo. Timmy bathed in all the cuddles and treats, culminating in a salmon birthday cake with cream on top. Jo took a photograph in the garden of me holding Timmy close to my heart, filled with gratitude and love for her long life and enduring friendship. I knew this might be her last birthday, so I savoured the moment, bending my head down to kiss her soft, marmalade coloured ears.

Later, when I looked at that photograph, I noticed the image was scattered with tiny spheres of semi-transparent light. Perhaps the camera had picked up some kind of dazzle. At that time, I had never heard of orbs.

Early the next year, though, Timmy became unwell. She had a couple of strokes and although the vet said she would be fine, I could see she wasn't, she was in pain and that I had to make the awful decision that all pet owners dread. Even if we've been through it before, it's always an impossible decision to make. We want to bargain with the universe to have more time and we hope against hope that the vet will come up with a miracle cure just at the last minute. We pray that our animal passes quietly in their sleep so we won't have to make that dreadful choice. I was sure that her end was here although ten per cent of me still held out hope.

Fortunately, my nice vet was available that very day so, at the appointed hour, my friends drove me to the surgery and I carried Timmy into the building in a blanket. It reminded me of her very first visit at just a few weeks old. So long ago. So much had happened. She was with me just after my medical training had finished and had stayed with me for twenty-one years until I was independent. I adored her and owed her so much.

The vet was very gentle and her voice was calm and soft. My two friends stood behind me and I could feel their support.

"Timmy is a very sick cat," she said. I felt myself beginning to tremble. "She has cancer of the jaw," she continued with professional calm. "You've done the right thing bringing her in. We need to end this pain now."

At least the decision wasn't mine to make anymore and I was so glad I hadn't delayed. This was outside my control. Timmy didn't seem afraid.

"Ready?" said the vet.

As soon as I whispered "Yes", Timmy's body went limp and, in the same moment, I saw a golden, cat-shaped mist leap free from her body into the air. Imagine a cat leaping from your arms, perfectly formed, but as a golden cloud. Her spirit leaped free and my arms remained embraced around her now empty body. It was the same experience I'd had with Beryl the hamster all those years ago. As I began to cry, my friends gathered round me, holding me tight. After a few moments, I quietened down enough to listen to what the vet was saying.

"Her decline has been very sudden," she said. "Take her body home and take your time. I just want you to know that we offer a cremation service. But don't worry about that yet."

It's times like this we need our friends and I don't think I could have got through this without them. It showed great courage on their part to be with me.

Back at home, I stroked Timmy's ears and looked at the pretty stripes on her tail. My friends were saying things like, "She had a good long life" and "It was for the best". It was helpful and I needed to hear it but found it impossible to respond with any coherence. I kept replaying the moment she'd turned to golden mist.

After a while, my friends suggested they go and get some chips in case I got hungry but didn't want to cook that night. I nodded, but I didn't want to eat anything.

Timmy's body was beginning to cool down. It made me shudder. Betty followed my friends to the door and, once they'd gone, she pottered back and tiptoed over her bed to get to the sofa. But instead of jumping up, she pointed her nose just to the right of me, where Timmy used to sit.

"I'm so sorry, Betty," I said quietly, "your sister has passed away."

Betty continued to point her nose towards the sofa to my right. She caught my eye and looked again. It was just like she used to do when she spotted a squirrel in the park. I used to call it pointing. I looked to my right. Betty wagged her tail. She was grinning, her mouth open and her ears perked up, her tail held high. It was as though she was trying to show me something my dim human eyes couldn't perceive. She continued to wag her tail and point her nose at the sofa. I patted the cushion in case she was asking permission to jump up.

"Okay," I said as brightly as I could.

I always said this to give permission to do something. She didn't budge. She just grinned at the sofa and wagged her tail. She wasn't paying Timmy's body any attention.

Was it possible?

"Can you see her?" Of course she couldn't. "Really?"

I didn't even know that animals could grieve never mind that they might be psychic. Rupert Sheldrake and Pamela Smart once published a study in the Journal of the Society for Psychical Research in which they concluded, "Not only do many dogs and cats seem to have better developed psychic powers that most people, but they provide good opportunities for repeatable research. Human subjects often get bored by doing repetitive tests for parapsychological experiments, but fortunately dogs do not get bored with being taken for walks, nor cease to be excited by their owners' coming home. The results of this survey show that pets with seemingly psychic powers are common."[5]

Science aside, many people believe that their pets have a sixth sense. We've all seen a cat staring at a wall. What are they seeing? Are they just having a vacant episode or can they see something we can't? I'm confident that Betty was trying to show me something that I couldn't see.

My friends arrived back with our chips and the moment was broken. I placed Timmy's body, wrapped up in the blanket, next to me on the sofa and didn't say anything about having seen her spirit leave her body or Betty trying to tell me that Timmy was visible to those with eyes to see. I just poked at my congealing chips with a fork. I tried a mouthful but I could barely swallow.

My friends kept talking to me, showing me such kindness and care. When they'd finished eating, they took my untouched plate of food and put everything in the kitchen. They washed up quietly and made me a cup of tea. Then they left me to it, saying I probably needed some time on my own to grieve. I nodded and thanked them.

When they'd gone, I knelt down with one hand on Betty's head and one hand stroking Timmy's back. What had I seen? And could Betty really see her?

In the old days, the deceased would be laid for a few days in an open coffin in our home. We used to wash their body and clothe it in their best clothes. We would brush their hair and make sure they looked as nice as possible. We would gather together as a family and make food and people would come to pay their respects. We would stare death in the face for a few days before committing the body to

---

[5]   https://www.sheldrake.org/research/animal-powers/
      psychic-pets-a-survey-in-north-west-england

the ground. Now, when someone dies, they're taken away and the next thing we see is the neat and tidy coffin with its pretty flowers. We're kept apart from death. Maybe we shouldn't be. Maybe life has become too clean and sanitised.

I decided to get a box for Timmy and surround her with her favourite toys and some flowers. Maybe I could write a poem for her. I would do this the old-fashioned way and maybe it would help me too. I also needed to make a plan for what to do about the body. I was concerned the crematorium would give me some ghastly mixture of all the animals that had died that day, rather than Timmy's ashes, so I decided to find out whether anyone did private cremations. I left Timmy wrapped in her blanket on the sofa and went to bed.

The next morning when I came downstairs there was no little bundle of fur in the kitchen eating her fishy flakes and jelly. Going through to the front room, I switched on the fire for Betty and gave her a cuddle. She was sitting with her head bent down and her face wet with tears. I didn't know that animals grieve. When I was young, most people used to think of animals as little furry robots without emotion, personality or the ability to feel pain or suffering in the same way that humans do. Anyone who has a pet knows they all have their own personalities, yet even that was considered bonkers by many. Any concept of animals being sentient and compassionate was unthinkable.

I was beginning to learn differently. I sat on the floor next to Betty and wrapped my arms around her. She leaned her head against my shoulder and we wept quietly together.

After a while, I persuaded her to have some breakfast and then took her out for a little walk. When we got back, I nestled Timmy's body in her blanket in a cardboard box and collected together her favourite toys and some flowers from the garden. Then I composed a poem for her and found a local farm on the Internet where they did private pet cremations. I was to take her in three days' time.

It so hard to let go, isn't it?

One of the things I struggled with is the totality of death. It's brutal. When we lose a human, at least we have objects and heirlooms to remember them by, maybe a favourite ornament or book. With an animal, we're left with virtually nothing and this is hard. Yes, we have memories that we can hold in our hearts forever, but I so wanted something permanent to keep.

I asked Timmy if it was all right for me to take one of her pure white whiskers. Then of course I felt silly for asking. She wasn't going to answer me. As soon as I'd snipped one off with my scissors, I knew I'd made a mistake, as though I'd violated her body. I felt dreadful. The only thing I could do was give the whisker back so I got some tape and stuck it onto the poem I'd written and placed it back inside the box with her.

This made me feel a bit better but I could tell that I was close to the edge. I was far too sensitive a person to have pets. I loved too deeply and grief always tore me apart. I carried the box upstairs and placed her in the bedroom, deciding to spend time with her whenever I needed to over the next few days.

When I went back downstairs again, Betty was still showing signs of distress and clearly missing her sister. Then I had a brainwave and fetched Timmy's favourite cushion from her bed. She'd had it for years. I placed it in Betty's bed so that she would have Timmy's scent for a while, then I climbed in next to her and hugged her. She rested her head on my shoulder again and leaned her full body weight against me as we held each other. After a few minutes, I sat up with my back aching from the bent over posture. That's when I noticed something incredible.

Right by one of Betty's paws was one of Timmy's whiskers. It was white. It was perfect. And freely given. I sobbed my thanks to the universe. The rational part of my mind said this was simply random chance and that it must have fallen from the cushion. But it didn't feel like that. It felt like a gift from Timmy.

Russell and Richard, two friends I'd met through my musical hobbies, had agreed to be with me for the day of the cremation. They'd both known Timmy for years and knew how much she meant to me. It seemed weird to have a pet cremation service in the countryside but every pet owner surely wants to know that the ashes they get back are the right ones, so it was worth the journey.

When the day arrived, I let Betty have one last look at Timmy and Richard drove me to the farm gently, not expecting me to talk. Russell met us in the car park and gave me a kind of sideways hug which, almost comically, included Timmy and the box. Nobody spoke. My lips were trembling as I knocked on the door. The farmer answered and took us to a workshop next to a barn where I noticed all sorts of silly details like the cobwebs in the corner and the lovely rounded wooden handles on the tools by the door. I noticed the watering can and the flowerpots. There was a smell of hay and silage and the air was cold. I clutched my box.

"I just have a few forms for you to sign," he said, his voice soft and gentle. He must have seen this kind of grief many times before.

I blindly filled in the forms, my eyes blurry with tears. They were terms and conditions documents that I didn't care about. As long as Timmy's body was treated with respect, that's all I wanted. It took every ounce of my courage to hand her over to him. It was as though I was ripping my own chest open and handing him my heart, but I had to do it. He took the box very gently and handed me a piece of paper.

"It's a poem," he said. "I thought you might find it useful."

"Thanks." I couldn't make sense of the words so I folded the paper and put it in my pocket.

"You can wait in the fields," said the farmer. "It'll be about an hour."

A few moments later, my friends and I were walking across a field of cows, over a stile and into a field that looked empty and quiet. Beautiful countryside flowed away in all directions, hills and fields and trees. The sky was clear. We lit some incense and poured some milk into plastic glasses, toasting Timmy's memory and sharing stories about her. I told my patient friends all about her kittenhood, finding the happy memories soothing. We talked about Betty's arrival and how the two of them had finally become such good friends.

As I eventually fell silent, two black and white farm dogs joined us. Although they seemed friendly, they didn't want to play or be stroked. I found comfort in their presence and didn't think anything strange was happening at this point. I was glad of their company.

A moment later, a horse walked over to us, followed soon by a second. There we stood, with the sound of birds in our ears, surrounded by animals like something out of a feel-good, magical animal movie. The horses came very close and allowed me to stroke their necks and faces.

I'd had this kind of help from a horse before, after my mother died. I was taking a walk one summer evening, still feeling fragile and needing some nature to calm me down. I was near a field just on the outskirts of the city so decided to climb a stile and sit by the roots of an ancient oak for a while. As I put my head in my hands and let the tears flow, I heard the sound of heavy hooves coming slowly towards me. Glancing up, I saw one of those huge horses with a long straggly mane and muddy legs. It came right up to me, very quietly, and lowered its head to the point where its velvety nose almost brushed against my hair. I looked into its deep brown eyes and stroked its face. The horse didn't move away, it just stood there with its neck bent down towards me, its head next to mine.

This gentle, intimate contact broke the dam of emotion in me and I'd cried, holding onto this gentle beast until the tears subsided. It was the best grief counselling I'd ever had. We'd stayed there in silence together for a little longer and then the horse lifted its head, snorted softly and turned, walking slowly back across the field.

As I grieved for Timmy now, I was being comforted in the same way by two horses, two dogs and two humans. I gazed up at the sky and had the distinct impression that there were creatures, animals and other beings, just above the trees, playing happily. Everything seemed beautiful and harmonious and just as it should be. Of course, I knew it was probably just my imagination but it was pleasant and I was glad my mind was finding some way of getting through this difficult time.

When we felt we'd waited long enough, I thanked the horses and dogs and we clambered back over the stile into the next field and walked towards the farm. As we went in single file, I heard my friends' laughter behind me. I turned and couldn't believe my eyes. Walking in procession, nose to tail behind us, was a long line of cows, following us all the way to the far edge of the field as if joining in our ceremony. Dogs, horses and cows.

My mind reeling, I joined in the laughter, feeling a wonderful sense of relief. I didn't understand what was happening. All I knew was that there was magic in the air.

NINE

The Rainbow Bridge

When we got back to the farm, Timmy's ashes weren't ready for collection. The farmer said there was a café a short drive down the main road. I didn't really want to be indoors with noisy strangers but we couldn't stand around in the cold any longer. And my back was beginning to ache. The café was one of those places with greasy bacon sandwiches for lorry drivers and people pausing their journeys to have a quick break. We sat by a long window next to the main road and I ordered a hot chocolate.

As I hugged my drink, the magical elation from earlier dissolved and I began to feel terrible again, my skin crawling. I wanted to go back to the farm and grab Timmy back. Stop it all happening. I knew I couldn't do that so I just sat there and tried not to think. I didn't want to talk. I knew that, very soon, I'd have to get a grip and take Timmy's ashes home and I wasn't quite sure how I was going to do that.

"Look out of the window," said Richard, patting my arm to get my attention.

I did a double take. One of the Collie dogs from the farm was right by the window on the grass verge outside. He was standing rigid, his nose pointing back down the road like a soldier on duty. How did he get here? And why? A feeling of calm came over me, a calm that surrounded the dog and myself in a quiet space slightly away from normal life. I began to relax as I gazed at the dog.

'It's all right.'

They weren't words exactly. It was as though I could hear the dog's thought, translated instantly into words in my mind.

'We're taking care of her now.'

These thoughts or concepts came straight from the dog to me.

'You've done your part.'

The dog didn't look at me once, it just kept staring down the main road towards the farm.

'Everything is all right. She's fine.'

I knew the communication couldn't have come from my imagination because it would have been beyond any belief system of mine to invent such a whimsical fantasy. I felt utterly astonished and completely at peace and I didn't understand why.

It's really difficult when the universe takes us down an Alice in Wonderland hole of non-reality. We want to believe our own experience yet, if we share it, we feel we'll be laughed at or, even worse, just humoured. But if we stay silent we could be denying ourselves the opportunity to grow. So we usually pretend everything is normal and conform to other people's ideas of what is sane, because it's uncomfortable to stand out from the crowd. It comes down to the kind of people we're used to being around and their beliefs. If I'd been in the company of people who call their dogs angels, or who are quite happy to accept that a messenger from God could inhabit an animal briefly, then I might have thought differently.

It seemed completely insane to me that this beautiful dog had found me in the field and then joined me at the café to give me a message. Was this a normal farm dog temporarily used by a higher being or was it a higher being itself? Even asking questions like this made me feel a little ridiculous. There was no way I was going to tell anybody so I just tucked it away in my mind to be looked at later.

"Maybe we should go back now," said Russell, glancing at his watch.

The farmer greeted me with a little wooden box with Timmy's name written on a brass plaque and the Chinese script for 'beautiful cat' as I'd asked. His expression was serious and sympathetic.

"You can pay me by cheque later," he said. "Just go home and rest. I can see how much she meant to you."

As soon as I held the casket in my hands, I felt a wave of peace come over me. I didn't speak much on the way back and Richard, sensitive to my mood, left me on my own once we got to my house, which is what I wanted. I put the casket on the mantelpiece, switched on the gas fire and cuddled Betty. It was just us now.

When I hung my coat up, I rediscovered the poem given to me by the farmer. It was by an anonymous author and was about the pain of making that difficult decision when an animal becomes seriously ill. It was a sweet poem but clearly written for a dog. I wanted to write my own version for Timmy so I settled down with a notebook and a glass of whiskey while I put some words together. I kept the early part the same as the original and then added my own words. This is my version.

> *If it should be that I grow frail and weak,*
> *and pain should keep me from my sleep,*
> *this day, more than all the rest,*
> *your love and friendship stand the test.*
>
> *Take me where they'll stop the pain*
> *and with me to the last remain.*
> *Hold me, gentle, special friend.*
> *Hold me 'til I reach the end.*

Hold my trusting, tiny paw.
Hold me 'til I breathe no more.
Even though your heart cries, No!
When the time comes,
let me go.

You've cared for me for all these years,
so try to put aside your fears
and do one last, brave deed for me.
Hold me,
love me,
set me free.

Sniffing, I searched the Internet to see how other people coped with pet loss and came across a website called Rainbows Bridge.[6] This is a place where you can register your animal in a memorial, take part in a candlelit ceremony every Monday and chat about how you feel with kind and supportive animal lovers. I stayed on there for a long time, feeling heard. I wish now that I'd shared my spiritual experiences with these people and I'm sure they would have been understanding, but I didn't think of it at the time.

Most people are probably familiar with the Rainbow Bridge now but I didn't really know about it at the time. Now, having had the crazy experience at the cremation with all the animals, that sense of joy in the sky and then the compassionate, angelic mind blast from the dog, I was beginning to wonder.

If we can allow ourselves to think in new, nonjudgmental ways, it can feel like shedding an old skin that has become too tight and restrictive.

---

[6]   www.rainbowsbridge.com

But it can also feel risky. How much judgement and decision-making is learned from others and how much is truly our own? From the moment we're born, we absorb the rules of the world. As young children, we learn important lessons like 'Don't run across the road' and 'Don't put your hand on hot things', that sort of thing. These lessons become a part of the fabric of life, so much so that we internalise them completely. These examples are life-saving and sensible yet there are many that are to do with manners and social cohesion, like 'Say please and thank you', 'Don't be late' and 'Don't eat all the cake'. These become internalised just as strongly as the life-saving ones.

These internalised rules are called introjects. They become so much part of us that we don't question them. However, introjects such as 'Men have to be strong' are simply ideas from previous generations and can lead to negative behaviours, in this case like toxic masculinity. And social media is having a huge impact on the internal rules of young people today. We all seem to be looking to others to work out how to behave.

By allowing myself to voice my feelings in my diary without judgement, I felt liberated. However, it was going to be a while before I would have the courage to talk to others.

For the next few days, Betty continued to react as though Timmy was still around. She'd wag her tail and run along the garden, looking up at the fence. In the evening, she'd sometimes point at the sofa. Have you ever seen an animal do that? Perhaps it's not that unusual.

A week later, Betty came running into the kitchen wagging her tail and indicating for me, in a sheepdog kind of way, to follow her into the garden. It had been raining hard and a beautiful rainbow arced over the whole sky. Betty stayed by my side as I watched in awe.

Just as at the cremation, I could sense Timmy 'up there' but this time it felt like she was flying away from me towards the rainbow, radiating joy and excitement. It was just like when I took my first trip as a Girl Guide, sitting in the back of the van with all my friends, waving goodbye to my parents. I was being driven away from them and yet I was filled with excitement, going on an adventure.

The rainbow began to shrink so I went upstairs to look at it from the bedroom window. It was now fading down to a quarter arc. I gasped. It appeared to be ending over the roof of the veterinary surgery. I looked at the clock. It was 5:15, precisely the time she had died exactly a week before.

I sank to the ground, stunned. Then I remembered that lecture I'd heard at the Buddhist Centre all those years ago, in which Lama Chime Rinpoche had talked about highly accomplished meditators spontaneously leaving their body as rainbows at the point of death. I've found out since that there have been documented cases even in the modern day of this and the Buddhist community takes it very seriously.

Many people talk about seeing rainbows after someone has died. I didn't think for a moment that Timmy was a high lama, however special she was to me, but the location of the rainbow and the time of its ending seemed to be beyond all coincidence.

Did I have the courage to trust that maybe I'd been wrong about the universe all my life?

Not everyone has the same introjects because they depend on our culture but every society has them. If one of your rules is 'Don't stand out from the crowd' and then you start having psychic experiences with animals, then life can become a little bit uncomfortable… To challenge an introject is to challenge the very fabric of our being. It takes time and courage. I had now to concede that there was a dimension subtly joined to this one, a spiritual world where animals were welcomed and where they could play in joy. This was a huge leap forward.

A couple of days later, I heard an advertisement on the radio asking for local stories. It was called *Inside Lives* and, to have a chance of being broadcast, they asked people to send in a small piece of writing. I wanted so much to tell the world about Timmy and how amazing she'd been, so I scribbled down the outline of the story of her gift of the white whisker. I was amazed when I got a call telling me that I had been chosen.

I needed to have the final draft of the story ready within a week so I didn't have much time. I put it together, line by line, as I tearfully washed Timmy's food bowls and cleaned out her litter tray. Once in the recording studio, a lady explained that I would be given a microphone and asked to read. My heart was thumping at the thought that my love for Timmy was going out across the airwaves and, when it came to the live recording, my voice cracked with emotion. I glanced up at the lady and she signalled for me to carry on.

A week later, I was in the kitchen, listening to the radio. I knew when the programme was going to be aired and had told all my friends who had known and loved Timmy.

"Welcome to Inside Lives with BBC Radio Derby..."

Life in the city with its petrol fumes and graffiti was getting to me and I'd noticed Betty still had her head lowered a lot of the time on our walks. She seemed low in spirits and I assumed she was missing her sister. Maybe it was time for a change?

I'd noticed a house for sale in my price range on the edge of the countryside with far-ranging views to the north so I made an offer and put my house on the market. The new place was still close enough to my neighbours for us to continue meeting up so it wasn't too a scary a change. My house sold within twenty-four hours and pretty soon

I was packed and ready to move. A couple of friends hired a van and helped me with all my boxes and furniture while Betty pushed at my knees, keen to get inside and explore our new home.

Having thanked my friends profusely for all their hard work, Betty and I set off to explore an area of grass surrounded by blossoming cherry trees in front of the house. The air was fresh. Betty's tail was wagging so hard it was almost going in a circle. I could see that moving here had been a good idea because there were many little walks to choose from. Crossing the Green and taking one of the random side roads, we came across a parade of shops – a hairdresser, a pizza place and a branch of the vet that I already used so I nipped in to introduce myself.

"Oh hello, who do we have here?" said the receptionist. She was sitting at a desk surrounded by dog treats. I liked her instantly.

"This is Betty," I said in that especially proud way parents do. Betty jumped up and put her paws on the desk.

"Would she like a snack?"

I stayed quite a while, talking all things dog and cat and telling her all about Timmy. I could see we were going to become firm friends and was also pleased to find out that my usual vet worked at this branch too.

The next morning, after breakfast, we went to explore the nearby fields with views over Derbyshire. All along the grass verge and in the fields, rabbits hopped and bounced in the sunshine. Betty had never seen rabbits before. Her ears were pricked and her tail was held so high it almost curled in a spiral over her back.

But sadly, Betty now had arthritis in her elbows. The vet said I could let her run on an extended lead but that it would be harmful now for her to run free and do her usual spinning and jumping. No-one seemed to have mentioned the arthritis to Betty, though, who still leaped out of bed and ran to the door if anybody came to visit.

I settled into the new house slowly, unpacking boxes a few at a time. It felt strange being there without Timmy and I kept thinking how much she would have enjoyed catching all the mice in the countryside. I missed the weight of her on my legs at night and her cuddles, but the new place helped lift my spirits.

Something strange was going on, though. I kept getting a vague sense of a cat on the stairs and in the garden. It was just a feeling or the blur of an image in the corner of my eye that disappeared when I looked closely. I didn't tell anybody about it until I actually saw it one night.

I was settling to sleep, not thinking about anything otherworldly. In fact I was busy planning what to do about the peeling wallpaper, when I felt a cat jump on the bed. At first, I thought it was a real cat, maybe one that had managed to get into the house by mistake, but there was enough light coming in from the streetlights outside for me to see this was no ordinary cat. Besides, I didn't have a cat flap. It was a dark cat shape, outlined in dull gold, padding silently towards me and settling by my pillow.

An astral cat? A ghost cat?

This wasn't Timmy, it just didn't feel like her. My mind reeled. Swallowing my shock, I tentatively put my hand onto its back to stroke it but I couldn't feel any contact. Having never met a spirit cat before, I had no idea what to do so I just continued to stroke the golden outline and talk to it. I crooned to this little cat for quite a while, wishing it peace and happiness. Whether I was really communicating or not, I had no idea. I hoped it was listening and was going to be okay. A human being I could understand, but what would cause an animal to be stuck down here? After a while, it faded away and I went downstairs to make some chamomile tea and tell Betty all about it.

I knew the previous owners of the house had pets so had this cat perhaps belonged to them? My new neighbour, a keen animal lover, had told me that they hadn't looked after their animals well, often leaving the dog in the tiny yard so long that it scratched the plastic of the back door to get back in and chewed its bed to pieces in distress. Some people don't deserve to share their lives with animals. Had this cat died at the house and stayed there rather than following its owners? And why hadn't it flown up to the Rainbow Bridge like Timmy?

The next day, I mentioned it to Jon, one of my new singing friends. He told me that his cat often visited him from the other side. This seemed quite normal to him but to me it was astounding. I also mentioned it to the veterinary nurse, whom I visited whenever Betty and I went past on our walks, and she said she regularly saw her cat as real and solid as it had been in life. It wasn't extraordinary at all to her, whereas I couldn't believe I was even having conversations like this.

On the one hand, I was beginning to accept that our own beloved pets may visit us to show us that they're all right, but why would we get a visit from a cat that we don't know? Ghosts and spirits are different. Spirits are those that have crossed over peacefully and happily and are free to come back to tell us they're okay, to give us a warning or to protect us. On the other hand, ghosts are beings that are trapped on this plane for some reason. I felt as though this particular spectral cat was seeking comfort but I never saw it again so I hope it found peace.

For many years, I'd put all my experiences down to coincidence or hallucination. However, the evidence was really mounting up now. It was either nonsense or I was a little bit psychic. And if I was, did I have to accept the possibility of mediumship and all the paranormal stories in the Bible?

What if it was all true?

I'd never given credence to any of it before but cracks were now appearing in my defences. One 'golden mist event' could be put down to hallucination or an overactive imagination but two, followed by rainbows, telepathic dogs and ghost cats... well that was amounting to a convincing level of evidence.

I was too far away from the Buddhist centre where I'd met Lama Chime Rinpoche and I hadn't been doing my meditation regularly since it's hard to motivate yourself when you're on your own. I was willing to accept there was a bigger picture and I wanted to know more. But I had no idea how.

If I were to accept, even for a few seconds, that any of those Bible stories were true, then it would change everything. If Jesus turned up in the middle of a busy shopping centre on a Saturday morning, doing miracles, I imagine it would cause a bit of a kerfuffle. Even diehard sceptics may change their minds. I think I would, at that point. I sort of envy those who can take things on faith, or who change their beliefs after one simple revelation, because I like to scrutinise everything.

Thinking about all this and looking for answers, I came across a fascinating YouTube interview with Joanna Lumley and the Dalai Lama. She asked him whether he believed in Heaven and he said that he did, but not quite in the usual way. He was talking about the Pure Land, or Dewachen as it's called in Tibetan. This is a land of bliss into which we can be reborn, rather than descending to the earthly realms again where we're destined to suffer, grow old and die. It's still not the ultimate, illuminated oneness of full enlightenment but it seems like a lovely place to be, and many Buddhists pray that their loved ones go to the Pure Land after death.

I clicked on another video where the Dalai Lama was talking to a group of people in a marquee about religious tolerance. He advised that if you were a Buddhist but had no access to a Buddhist community, then you should look within your own culture and find something to enable you to continue your spiritual journey with others. He emphasised that community was important.

My ears pricked up at this. I'd rejected the Church at a young age but if the Dalai Lama was suggesting that Christianity in its many forms was a viable path on someone's spiritual journey, then who was I to argue? Maybe the idea was worth investigating, although I still really struggled with the history of misogyny, patriarchy and homophobia in Christianity, not to mention the appalling and violent behaviour of the Church over the centuries.

When I asked Barbara what she thought about this, she said, "JC's okay, but I have a problem with the Church." That was interesting. I might have thrown the baby out with the bathwater. What if there was truth to be found hidden within the stories written over all those hundreds of years? She had called Jesus 'JC' like she knew him intimately. Well, if he was okay by Barbara and the Dalai Lama, then maybe it was time for me to do some researching.

The nearest church was in one of the suburbs of the city. It was pretty and old-fashioned, not just in appearance but in the style of its services as well. I knew they had a choir and I loved singing. Fortunately, the church was inclusive, meaning it was friendly to people of any colour, race, orientation and so on, which made me feel a bit more positive about it.

It was there that I met Ann. I was introduced to her during coffee time after one of the services and, just like with the golden puppy and Betty, I felt like I'd known her all my life (and possibly beyond). I'd never met her before yet she seemed as familiar to me as family. We chatted away like old mates as we sipped our rather strong coffee and ate our biscuits, almost as though we were catching up on old times rather than a first meeting.

I joined the choir as planned and sat at the front in my robes feeling slightly fraudulent, singing hymns and anthems. Yet I was surprised at how similar the lessons were to those of the Buddhist scriptures. Sitting there felt just like sitting in the Buddhist retreat centre, where

I'd heard about rainbows and enlightenment and kindness. Now, I was listening to the story of a man who taught love, compassion and kindness to others. A man who could calm storms and, after his death, walk through walls.

I realised that there's a lot in both religions to help us become the best version of ourselves. Whatever the big picture, and whoever is right about it all, we can only do our best with what we have in the time given to us.

TEN

Your Paw in My Hand

The following summer, my new friend Jon asked whether I would like to take him on as a lodger. He loved animals, chocolate and Star Trek as much as I did, so I agreed. This gave me much needed company and financial help as I was still unable to work. In fact, a few months after he moved in, my health took a turn for the worse. Despite being careful, I'd done too much one day and the nerve pain in my face had returned.

The hospital physiotherapist said that, after my car accident, my brain had not wired up properly and this was leading to the problems with my muscles and fascia. I was given some gentle neck movements to do and told that, if they didn't work, the doctors would have to paralyse some of my muscles in order to encourage my body to begin working properly. This, she said, was a last resort and she hoped they wouldn't have to do it.

Fortunately, the movements worked after a few weeks and the pain eased down from critical to just about manageable with drugs. However, I was forced to reduce my activities for a while and felt like a bird in a cage, watching others live life while I rested and took gentle walks like an old lady. Whenever I lay on my back to ease my spine, Betty would lean gently on my legs just enough to give comfort.

It was during this difficult time that a new cat came into my life. I once read a wonderful short story about a woman who was very lonely and was reaching a low point in her life when a tiny kitten came into her garden. It came into her house and adopted her, so she soon gave up wondering about where it had come from and they lived a long and happy life together. You can imagine how good that would make you feel, as though that cat had been sent to you in a miraculous way. When the lady died peacefully, another person in the same street was unhappy and an identical kitten turned up in their garden. At the end of the story, we see that the kitten was really an angel.

Of course, the cat about to enter my life was probably not sent from Heaven but she might as well have been. Although I didn't think I could help her at first because of my own health problems, things turned out perfectly.

It was late one evening when Jon and I were watching television and the phone rang. I immediately recognised the voice of Jo, my past neighbour from when I was married, who'd been living in York with her new boyfriend.

"I know we haven't spoken in ages," she said, "but I need your help." Her voice sounded ragged and anxious, almost breathless. I couldn't imagine what could be causing her such distress. "It's Dolly," she went on.

I remembered the long-haired tortoiseshell cat who used to sit on the dividing wall between our houses, the cat who wouldn't let any adult touch her and who would never come indoors.

"What's the matter? Is she sick?"

"Can you take her?" said Jo. "Can you give her a home? I'm on my way to you now. I just stopped to ring you. I'm only a few minutes away. If anybody can manage to give her a home it's you. You're the right person."

"But I've got Betty."

At the sound of her name, Betty looked up at me and tipped her head on one side. She probably thought I was organising a party for her.

"Dolly was all right with Freya, my lurcher," said Jo. "Sort of. I don't know what else to do."

Betty wagged the tip of her tail.

"Well, we can give it a try."

"Thank you. I haven't the heart to take her back to the rescue centre. She'd be so unhappy there."

Jo arrived a few minutes later with Dolly in a carrier. Jon and I murmured gentle hellos to the terrified ball of fluff. We took Dolly upstairs and shut the bedroom door before opening the carrier. Something dirty and ragged shot out and dived under the bed. Two eyes blinked at me, reflecting in the light, eyes that held a quiet sadness and a deep sense of betrayal.

"How did she get like this?" I asked.

"She's been living under a shed for the last year," said Jo.

"What? That's awful. Maybe we should leave her to settle for a while," I said. "Let's have a cup of tea and let her calm down. We can talk about what we're going to do."

Dolly was terrified. Her distrust of humans was hardly surprising. I would be afraid if I'd been abandoned in a cardboard box by the canal while my kittens died and then been so scared that I had to hide under a shed for a year with only a dirty, cloth mouse for company.

The next morning, I made a terrible mistake. I'd opened the window a crack, just enough to ventilate the room while I went to have a shower. I thought I'd slotted it properly so that it couldn't be opened more than a centimetre but when I came back into the bedroom the window was wide open and Dolly was nowhere to be seen.

I panicked, threw on some clothes and took Betty with me outside to see if she could find Dolly's scent. She led me down to some garages on the other side of the Green. It was quite clear Dolly was there somewhere so I leafleted the area. Three weeks went by and I began to believe that she'd gone forever. I felt so utterly guilty to have failed this beautiful animal and now she was going to be at the mercy of the elements. Was nothing going to go right for this cat? Why is it that terrible things happen to beautiful people and animals and yet the nasty people of the world seem to get off scot-free? It just isn't fair.

Then, one happy day, I got a phone call.

"Hello. I live nearby and I think I've seen your cat," said a lady. "It was your comment about her having a tail like a fox that made me realise it was her. I live at the bottom of the Green and she was behind my back gate, near my garage. I've managed to get her into my garden. I'll give you my address so you can pick her up."

I was a bit shocked when the lady answered the door because she looked angry. Her lips were a thin line and her eyes were dark. Another woman was sitting on the sofa, frowning and looking accusingly at me. I had no idea why, so I tried to ignore it. I just wanted Dolly back. I stayed by the door and looked beyond them into the dining room where I could see a dark shape hiding in a corner. I knelt down and opened my blanket.

"Dolly," I called. She didn't move. The two women stared at me, their faces like stone. "Dolly, come on, it's okay."

I held the blanket wider. Dolly hesitated for a second then seemed to make up her mind. To my relief and delight, she came out from the corner and ran towards me, her sad, round eyes locked onto mine. She galloped straight into the blanket and clung to me, allowing me to scoop her up. I held her skinny body close to my heart and burst into tears. I knew at that moment that I would go to the ends of the Earth to protect her.

"Oh my goodness," said the lady. "I'm so sorry."

Sniffing back my tears, I looked up. Both women were crying along with me. They were leaning forward, smiling and wiping their eyes as Dolly rested quietly in my arms.

"What do you mean?"

"We were really angry with you," she said. "We thought you must be a terrible, cruel pet owner."

"Why?"

"Because, when we finally saw Dolly up close, we saw how awful her fur was and how scared she was. We decided that if she was afraid of you, we wouldn't allow you to take her. But when she ran into your arms, we could see that she—" Her voice faltered as she dabbed her eyes with a tissue.

I told them Dolly's story, watching their eyes widen as they gradually understood about her terrible life and how Betty had helped to find her.

Dolly settled in fine. She loved being cuddled by Jon who had a calm and gentle approach with her. I even made her a den in the garden, protected by a tarpaulin. Last but not least, I crawled under my bed to retrieve her dirty red mouse. I wasn't sure whether to give it a wash or not. Did it smell of her previous year of torment under the old shed or did it represent security?

Betty was wonderful with Dolly. She was usually such an inquisitive and bouncy dog yet she seemed to understand that Dolly was delicate and knew just what she needed. Animals are far more intelligent and caring than many people think.

Anyone who has animals knows that there comes a point when you suddenly notice that they're getting older. Their muzzle has more grey hairs, they're slower on their feet and may be having trouble with their teeth. It's easy to love a puppy or kitten and I'm always deeply saddened by people who reject animals when they get older. I have loved all my animals to the very end, even if they got grumpy with me sometimes.

One day, I got a glimpse of what it would feel like to be without them. We had all been living happily together for a while but then one day Betty developed a limp and had to stay in hospital to have X-rays. It was an uncomfortably quiet day without her in the house.

In Buddhism, one of the important teachings is that we should try to live in a state of spacious awareness in which our little boat of life isn't capsized by the good or the bad. Rather, we surf the waves that come our way with equanimity and ease. Well, that's the theory anyway but I wasn't very good at it.

A quick look on the Internet told me that dogs of mixed breed generally live between fourteen and sixteen years. Betty was twelve, which gave her two more years at worst and four at best. I couldn't get my head around this because I just wanted her here on Earth with me forever. I didn't know then the huge role that Betty would play in my life after she'd gone, thereby nudging me another step on my spiritual journey.

When I went to collect her from the vet, I was told that she'd snapped a little piece of bone from her elbow and would need to rest for a while and have doggy physiotherapy. Fortunately, by the next morning she was no longer disorientated and over the next few weeks her elbow mended and we were back to walking in the rabbit field.

I don't know why, but she would not accept my new-found Reiki skills. She was normally always up for cuddles and contact but every time I approached her with my hands open to give Reiki, she would move away or gesture with her head that she wasn't interested. Was it my hand position or was she simply not interested in that kind of thing? And if it was the latter, what was she detecting and why did she not want the help? I know we don't always have to accept help when it's offered, but it was interesting that one animal would welcome it and another not. Dolly wasn't interested either!

One morning, I came down for breakfast and saw something that I'd been wanting to see for a long time: Betty was sharing her bed with

Dolly, just as she had with Timmy for all those years. My eyes filled with tears as I gazed at them. It showed just how far Dolly had come, learning to trust the world so much that she could sleep indoors, curled up paw to paw with a dog.

She was a lot more trusting with humans too. She preferred people who approached her with a quiet voice and no expectations and she would sniff their fingers before deciding whether they were suitable to be allowed to stroke her. But she didn't run away in the old panicky way when a stranger came round. She was healing. Then, after a happy time lodging at my house, Jon eventually fell in love and moved away. He'd been brilliant with Dolly and I might not have been able to take her on without his help at the beginning. Both animals and I missed him immensely.

As Dolly gradually relaxed, she developed a habit of poking her tongue out to express affection. It was her way of giving a kiss and I would always return the gesture to show that I loved her too. She would catch my eye, hold my gaze for a second and then out would pop her cute pink tongue. She did the slow blink sometimes too, but the tongue became a kind of signature.

One day, she was in the garden and Betty was with me in the living room. Betty got up from her bed by the fire and went to the back door. Before I could get there to open it for her, she turned and poked her tongue out at me then looked at the door again. When I looked through the glass portion of the door, there was Dolly, waiting to come in. Betty had used the gesture to name her sister. Do researchers know that this is possible? Is it a recorded phenomenon? It blew my mind that a dog, no matter how intelligent, could find a way of naming her feline friend and communicating that to a human.

A couple of years went by. I went to the church when I could and even joined in some social activities. I felt comfortable enough there and was happy that no-one asked me about my beliefs. There were still swathes of the religion I couldn't get my head around, but Ann and I enjoyed deep and meaningful conversations over lunch regularly and life was as good as it could be.

However, one night in late October I was jolted from sleep by the sound of Betty whimpering. Something was wrong. My heart thumped as I grabbed my dressing gown, fumbled for my slippers and ran downstairs. Betty was staggering and lurching around, bumping into the furniture, trying to find the way out. I opened the back door for her and watched in horror as she half fell across the threshold, staggered into the garden and collapsed. Despite my bad back, I summoned the strength of a mother with a wounded child and helped her onto the grass. She kept wobbling and falling. The rain soaked through my dressing gown and slippers and my hair dripped around my face as I supported her while she had a wee.

Even complete non-believers pray when things get really bad. I threw my religious doubts to the wind and prayed out loud, desperately.

"Please God, help her! Please help her! Oh God, what's happening?"

I was surprised the neighbours didn't look to see what the disturbance was about. Still, when things get this scary we don't care what other people think, we just call out for help. I placed my hands on Betty's shoulders and talked to her quietly, telling her how much I loved her, telling her that everything would be okay. This seemed to calm her a little but her legs gave way again and I had to hold her weight as she did a poo on the lawn.

Once safely indoors, she continued to lurch and pant and shake. We were both soaked through so I put the central heating on then tried to dry her and get her into her bed, but she was too stressed. It was clear she couldn't see properly. I offered her a carrot but she didn't want it. For the first time in fourteen years, she refused a carrot. I rang the vet who said it would be quicker to bring her in. Fortunately, Bill and John, two dear friends of mine, lived nearby and I knew they were often up late so I rang them. I couldn't do this alone and was relieved when Bill answered.

"I think Betty's dying," I gasped, barely able to get the words out. "I can't carry her."

"I'll be there in five minutes."

I offered Betty another piece of carrot and, to my massive relief, she took it. Her head was lopsided and it was clear she couldn't see properly as I had to hold the carrot right to her nose before she realised it was there.

Bill and John turned up in record time and they carried her to their car. I sat in the back, holding her draped across my lap, smelling her damp fur. I was too shy to say any potential goodbyes out loud but I beamed my love to her. By the time we got to the emergency vet she was able to walk unaided and looked a little more settled. I was just so relieved to see this and that she no longer had a wild look in her eyes.

It turned out she had a problem with her ears, a vestibular disorder that was affecting her balance. Fortunately she recovered, but the next summer she developed a new problem. During the day she seemed fine, but she became restless as it got dark. If I stroked her and talked to her quietly, she'd settle; but the minute I moved away, she'd sit up and whimper. This scared me. I could tell by the tone of the vet's voice when I spoke to her that this wasn't a simple problem to be solved with rest, exercise or medication. This was something more serious.

"This is something that can happen to older dogs," she said. "They become agitated as the light fades. I'd like you to stay with her until she's fully asleep. Just sit with her and talk to her until she falls asleep. Then you can go to your own bed. She'll be fine. If it gets worse, bring her in."

At six o'clock in the morning, Betty woke up and I took her outside into the front garden for a wee and then gave her breakfast and some painkillers. She seemed fine and all the agitation had gone. I had a quick shower and dressed, but by the time I came downstairs she was scratching at the front door, desperate to get outside again. This time she went straight to the wooden fence on the other side of the road and began pushing her nose under the bushes, searching frantically as though she'd lost a favourite toy or friend. She didn't seem connected to reality and I wondered whether she was hallucinating. I managed to persuade her to come back to the house and called the vet. We were seen immediately. The vet looked into Betty's eyes with a little torch.

"Oh dear," she said, meeting my gaze. "I'm so sorry."

I felt my knees go weak.

"This isn't what I thought it was," she said. "It's not dementia. She has something pressing on her brain. An aneurism. I can see it. She's got a bit of time – but only a few hours. Give her these tranquillisers and painkillers. They'll stop the agitation. Keep her happy and comfortable and come back at five-thirty this evening. Go and have the best day you can have."

I knew what this meant. She didn't need to say the terrible words. I didn't have to tell her how I felt. From the look on her face, I could see that she understood.

We all know that death is a natural part of life, yet it always comes as a terrible shock. We just want to go back in time to when our loved ones were younger. The pain of losing a pet can be as strong, if not sometimes stronger, than losing a relative or friend. Perhaps only other animal lovers understand this.

The tranquillisers worked quickly and by the time we were back in the car Betty looked completely normal. She sat next to me with her little red seatbelt harness on, looking ready for an outing. Although I felt numb and shaky, I knew I had to keep myself strong and positive for her sake. I decided to stop off at the rabbit field on the way home. It was only a few yards down the road so I parked up and put Betty on the flexible lead.

It was a sunny day with a few fluffy clouds in the sky. The field was awash with buttercups, yellow as far as the eye could see right up to the brow of the hill. Rabbits hopped along the hedgerow and cows chewed the cud nearby. The huge oak tree cast shade and flies buzzed over cowpats. Nature didn't seem to know that it was our last day.

Betty, clearly free from pain and anxiety due to the medication, bounced into the field like a puppy, even jumping over clods of grass in her enthusiasm. She looked ten years younger. I had the strangest sensation of being split in two, half of me reeling from shock and the other half smiling as she pranced about. She wasn't stressing about last night's confusion. She was simply happy to be with me right now among the flowers in the sunshine.

Later, we went out to the Green to sit on our special hill under the trees. She sat calmly by my side. I held the lead loosely in one hand and lay down on my back for a moment, looking up through the leaves of the trees above us. Betty looked down at me, her ears flopping forward. Her eyes were bright and kind. I told her how much I loved her but my grief felt like an avalanche threatening to engulf me. I wasn't sure I could hide it much longer. I wanted to bury my face in her fur and howl but I needed to stay positive for her sake and not scare her. At that moment, when I thought I was going to crack, Betty reached out her paw and placed it gently in my open hand. Her eyes held such love. It felt as though, even in those last precious moments, she was giving me comfort and strength.

She sat there, guarding me, with her paw in my hand.

Time closed in on that special moment. Everything became still. It was as though all the moments we'd ever shared, all the playful puppy games, all the holidays and parties, the quiet evenings by the fire and all the courage of the last six months, came together in a moment of peace and deep mutual gratitude. It was a moment I shall never forget. She showed me compassion just when I needed it most.

The human race considers itself superior because it can write poetry and make art. But how many people are capable of true unconditional love like animals are? It has become clear to me that they can give and receive compassion, that they can grieve and care for one another. Some people say that animals are often kinder than humans and I have to agree. On that little hill, with Betty's paw in mine, I felt a deep sense of peace and communion. I felt honoured to have enjoyed her love and affection for fourteen and a half years.

Finally, it was time to leave. I'd given Betty some kibble and fed Dolly her current favourite food. I knew that at any moment, Ann was going to come round. I needed her support and I'd asked her if we could visit more of Betty's favourite places before going to the vet. Just before we went into the vet's, I gave Betty a picnic in the car. She had all her favourite foods, salmon, cheddar cheese, carrots and banana. She sat there with me, gobbling it all with enthusiasm, her eyes wide with excitement. She even snorted with pleasure as she ate the salmon.

Then it was time.

Ann sat in the waiting room while the nurse, Betty and I went into the treatment room. The vet kept her voice low and observed Betty closely as she spoke to me about what would happen.

Staying by the side of your loved one while they pass away is extraordinarily painful. It's normal to want to run away and it feels like having your own heart ripped out. Yet being there is the greatest final gift you can give your animal, to be by their side, to hold their paw, to guide them gently as they transition. You've always been there for them for feeding time, walkies, cuddles on the sofa and playing with toys. You've looked after them when they were sick and played crazy games with them when they were well. Now it's time to do your one last, brave deed. To hold them, love them and let them go.

For some, of course, it may all really be too much or even damaging to health, so getting a friend who knows the animal well to take your place would provide that much-needed comfort instead.

I knelt down on the floor next to Betty, stroking her.

"Good girl. Good girl," I crooned. Her breathing slowed. My breathing slowed. I felt her drifting. I closed my eyes and drifted with her.

"You're doing really well," said the vet. "Keep talking to her."

"You're such a good girl. I love you so much. Good girl."

We merged together and I carried on talking to her, feeling us both melting down through the floor into a peaceful place. Then there was a sense of gentle expansion and dispersal, of floating away softly.

From far away, I heard the vet say, "She's gone."

ELEVEN

Angels in The Rabbit Field

"In all my years as a vet," she said, "I've never seen a bond so close as that between you and Betty." Her voice was gentle. "We used to watch you walk past together and point you out to the other customers. We used to say, 'That's how you should be with a dog'."

I was kneeling with one hand resting on Betty's back, one part of me in the room and the other part of me still with Betty. I found the vet's words a great comfort. I had no idea that we were being pointed out in a positive way as we took our daily walk and I'd always assumed that most people had an unbreakable bond with their dogs. The vet and the nurse continued to talk to me until I could focus and respond to them and I was so grateful to them for giving me as long as I needed. It was a timeless time and I had no idea how long it took for me to be able to speak.

Ann followed behind in her car and carried Betty into my house. I probably shouldn't have been driving but I needed to do this bit independently. I just wanted privacy. Although I wanted to be hugged and have cups of tea made for me, I also wanted to be alone. As soon as the door shut behind my dear friend, I lay down with my face against Betty's fur.

At first, Dolly kept her distance, staring with her big round eyes. She looked a bit scared yet she didn't run away. She didn't clean herself or purr or ask to go out into the garden. I stroked her back gently, trying to explain.

A pain started in my chest. Just a gentle ache at first but then it grew a bit stronger. I put my hand over my heart and took a few deep breaths. I'd had heartache in grief before but this felt different. I thought of my father, my aunt and my uncle, all of whom had died of heart disease. Surely, it couldn't actually be my heart, could it? Could grief do that to you? I tried to relax and felt the pain easing.

Suddenly, I experienced a strange sensation, like a mental nudge. I sat up. The nudge came again, this time clearly. There was a strong sense of Betty, of her joyful vibrancy. Then words came into my mind in an instant package just like they had when Timmy died and the farm dog had 'spoken' to me. The concept was translated instantly.

'Go outside. It will make you feel better.'

Was this the madness of grief or was it Betty? The voice felt different to the one I'd heard when I was a child, the one that told me to put on my plimsolls. This was a younger sounding voice, more energetic and eager.

I covered Betty's body with a blanket, told Dolly I would be back in a bit and went out into the front garden, eyes red and puffy, but I didn't care. I crossed the road to our special hill under the trees. How could I bear to walk across the Green without her lead in my hands and a poo bag in my pocket? I took a few stumbling steps forwards. A woman I'd never seen before was coming towards me along the path.

"Are you okay?" she said, stopping nearby.

I suddenly felt exposed and embarrassed. I wanted to do my usual British stiff-upper-lip thing but I couldn't hold it.

"No," I whimpered.

She marched up to me and enveloped me in a hug. A complete stranger holding me in her arms. My tears fell on her blouse as I told her what had happened. We broke apart and she looked me in the eye.

"I can't imagine the pain you're experiencing right now," she said. "I have a dog, a rescue dog, and he's not very well. I worry about him all the time. They're so precious aren't they?"

I just nodded because I couldn't speak any more. I wanted to collapse on the ground and yell out my grief. I wanted to scream.

"Where are you going?" she asked.

"Just for a walk. Nowhere."

"Would you like me to come with you?"

I nodded.

We walked just long enough for me to begin to speak without crumbling and by the time we parted company, I was no longer shaking. I was so grateful to that woman. Without that mental nudge that got me out of the house at exactly the right moment, I think I might have lost my mind. Could it be that Betty was looking after me? When I got back, I wanted to say a prayer for Betty, but I didn't know how. Going with my gut instinct, I lit some incense and found a YouTube video with a Buddhist prayer offering the deceased guidance.

In Tibetan Buddhism, the belief is that we go through an intermediate stage called the Bardo before our potential rebirth. According to their tradition, we may be lucky and go straight to the light after we die or we may wander about for a few days and experience colours and sounds which, they warn, could be frightening although are harmless, like dreams. We may see prospective parents in different places and the guidance given tells us which ones to avoid. The general advice is to keep going towards the light.

Most after-death prayers in Buddhism are for the person to have a happy rebirth, especially, if possible, in the highest realm, the Pure

Land. Beyond that is the light and this is where we all should be aiming. There is something similar to this in most religions.

I closed my eyes and breathed slowly and deeply. I was tense all over as though my body was trying to resist what was happening by sheer muscular effort. So I did my best to relax, letting the calm chanting flow over me, offering good wishes for a happy rebirth to all beings.

The next morning, there was a knock at the door. It was Russell, the guitarist who had helped at Timmy's funeral. He'd come to pay his respects and we stood together looking tenderly at Betty's body. I didn't really know what to say. There were no words.

"Are you all right?" he asked.

I just nodded. He knew I wasn't. He'd been with me during Timmy's funeral and he knew how much I loved my animals. He knew I was destroyed. I excused myself for a moment to go to the loo and as I climbed the stairs I heard him sigh.

"Aaah, lass," he said softly, his voice filled with loss and love.

Like many men, he didn't express his emotions outwardly, but this was a perfect eulogy. There was immense regret, grief, love, empathy and an acknowledgement of a wonderful creature in those words. Although it wasn't meant for my ears, it was incredibly helpful to hear. It was more like music than words. It said everything.

Russell and I drank mugs of tea and talked about Betty's life and about how I might handle the next few days. He was full of good advice, recommending that I keep my routine the same as much as possible: wake up at the same time, eat at the same time and introduce playtime with Dolly to replace the morning walk. Then, seeing I needed space, he gave me a hug and left me alone.

Fifteen minutes later, Bill and John arrived and we set off to the vet's. I held Betty's body on my lap in the back of their car, wrapped in a paw-print blanket and snuggled up to her gifts of carrots, toys and loving words. My brain gave up trying to cope.

I didn't know much about what Bill believed in. John and I had enjoyed many conversations about Buddhism and science, but all I knew about Bill was that he believed in angels. I plucked up courage to ask him a question.

"Bill, do you believe that people and animals fly free after cremation?" I asked. He caught my eye in the rearview mirror.

"Betty is already completely sorted," he said calmly. "But it does help once the body's been dealt with." I took a slow, shuddering breath. "She's already there," he continued, kindly. "She's learning all sorts of good stuff now. She's learning to communicate, seeing the big picture."

I decided to take his words on trust.

I knew I didn't have to hold myself together anymore because Betty was gone and my emotion wouldn't be frightening to her. I'd held myself together right up until her last breath and now I could let go. Except, I couldn't. I felt that if I let go properly I'd begin to scream and that would frighten everybody.

Each of us is in our own little boat on the river of life. Some of us have boats that leak due to no fault of our own and others are on rivers treacherous with the rocks and white water of loss. We can't control the ferocity of the water or the waves. We can only do our best and recognise when it's time to let go.

With great care, some nurses carried Betty's body in her blanket to the rear entrance of the surgery, placing her on the ground by the doorway.

"It's very busy here today," said the nurse. "It would be best to say goodbye here rather than inside. Take as long as you need. We'll come back in a bit."

I nodded. Bill and John stayed by the car although I could sense their solid, compassionate presence. Kneeling down on the doorstep, I placed my hand on Betty's head. I'd spent time the previous evening preparing what I wanted to say so that I wouldn't be lost for words at this crucial moment. Eternal love. Gratitude. A wish for her continued wellbeing.

A few moments later, the vet who'd helped liberate Betty from suffering came out of the back door to see me and I felt relief at seeing a familiar face. Gesturing to the carrot, the toy, the poem and the flowers, I asked whether it was all right for them to go with her. She squatted down by me and stroked Betty's ear.

"We don't normally allow anything to be included in the actual cremation." My heart clenched. "But I'm going to allow it in this case. Because it's Betty." I relaxed a bit and thanked her. "Don't worry now, she's running around free."

When they'd taken her from me, Bill enveloped me in a huge hug. It was over. Now I had to look after myself and Dolly although I had no idea how.

"I just got a message," said Bill. His voice was warm and infinitely caring. "I can hear that she's got plans for giving you something far greater than the ashes back. That, yeah, you can have that forever, but she's got something in store and they won't tell me what it is."

By 'they' I guessed he meant the angels. Did he have an open hotline to the spirit world? With no idea what to say, I clung to the words with hope and confusion. On the way home, I sat in the car in a state of numb shock as Bill continued to talk to me gently. His voice was comforting. He told me to watch out for any songs that came to my mind over the next few days as they could be messages. I blew my nose on yet another tissue.

"Do you ever doubt that all these things come from angels?" I asked.

"Occasionally," he said. His eyes met mine in the rearview mirror again. His face held a cheeky smile.

That surprised me. I'd always thought that people who had solid belief systems never wavered. Being with him was like being in the presence of an enormous, wise teddy bear. Comforting, reassuring and solid. I was so grateful to have him as a friend. John was wonderful too. He said he didn't know what to say when people cried, but he was a really good listener. When we got home, I thanked them and watched them drive away then closed my door. For a few heartbeats, there was silence. Utter silence.

Then Dolly came into the kitchen.

"Meep?"

Her round, fluffy face looked up at me, her eyes wide. I burst into tears of gratitude. She'd never welcomed me like that before, not with a 'meep'. Sometimes she would walk through with Betty when it was teatime but quite often she stayed quietly on her chosen cushion or out in the garden. Today's vocal welcome made all the difference.

I gave her a big fuss and some treats. Having gone through that experience with the white whisker, I knew for a fact that animals grieve. Betty had been Dolly's protector for years so I knew that Dolly would miss her sister immensely. I settled down to cuddle her.

Searching for something to help me, I looked for some guided meditations on YouTube. I'd let meditation slip for a while and I wasn't really sure what the lama had wanted me to do. Maybe there was another method that I could use now. I wanted something to relax me, to bring me comfort.

The first one that caught my eye had a lotus flower as a thumbnail. I clicked it and was blown away by the sheer beauty of a lilting Vietnamese song. I didn't understand a word of it of course but somehow it touched my heart. After the first stanza, a male voice then spoke some lines of poetry, presumably a translation of the song. I was mesmerised. Without knowing what his words meant, they nevertheless somehow touched me and made me smile despite my sadness. Below are a few lines from the original.

The End of Suffering *(from Graceful Passages)*

May the sound of this bell penetrate deep into the cosmos.
Even in the darkest spots, living beings are able to hear it clearly,
so that all suffering in them ceases,
understanding comes to their heart
and they transcend the path of sorrow and death.

Listening to the bell, I feel the afflictions in me begin to dissolve.
My mind calm, my body relaxed,
a smile is born on my lips.
Following the sound of the bell,
my breath brings me back to the safe island of mindfulness.
In the garden of my heart, the flowers of peace bloom beautifully.
(Thich Nhat Hahn)[7]

Meditation had never made me smile before. Thich Nhat Hahn was a Vietnamese Buddhist who had been a peace activist during the Vietnam war. I listened to some more of his videos and was hooked immediately. I wanted to learn more about this man, especially what he thought about death and the afterlife, so I explored further. Here's a short excerpt from one of his lectures to give you a flavour.

"Our greatest fear is that when we die we will become nothing. Many of us believe that our entire existence is only a lifespan beginning the moment we are conceived and ending the moment we die. We believe that we are born from nothing and when we die we become nothing. And so we are filled with fear of annihilation."

So far, fair enough. None of us want to be annihilated.

Then he went on to talk about there being no birth and no death and that we only suffer because we believe in these concepts. He talked

_____
[7]   https://youtu.be/NMab_IYY5lE

about how the clouds become rain and that rain falls into rivers and lakes. When the sun hits the water, it evaporates and rises once more as a cloud. So the cloud doesn't actually die, it just transforms itself into something different. This fits with the First Law of Thermodynamics, which states that energy cannot be created or destroyed, it can only be transmuted from one form to another. But his ideas left me feeling uneasy. Was he talking hard Physics: do we just melt into our constituent molecules and merge with the earth, or was there more?

I would imagine most people would prefer to fly up to Heaven in the arms of angels and meet their loved ones or find their pets at the Rainbow Bridge. There are so many stories of children remembering their past lives, especially in the first three or four years of life, and it's at this age that the Tibetan monks look for their reincarnated teachers. This implies an eternal soul. Did Thich Nhat Hahn believe in an eternal soul? I knew I was going to have to explore this a lot more if I were to understand truly.

Later that evening as I went upstairs to bed, Dolly was draped across the top of the sofa like a fluffy brown cushion. As I said my usual words of "See you in the morning," she gave me the same loving look that Betty usually gave. Her eye contact was steady and loving. I was amazed as she'd never done that before. Every night for fourteen and a half years, Betty and I had always shared a moment of loving eye contact as I'd said goodnight. Every single night. And now Dolly was taking over.

Once alone in my room, I rang Bill and John. Amongst a lot of nose-blowing and sobs, I managed to make it clear that I wasn't suicidal but I also made it clear that, without Dolly, I would probably simply slip away from the Earth because I felt so bad.

"You've got to stay here," said John. "People need you. Your friends need you." He paused for a moment. "And you've got to write something one day, something that's going to change everything."

141

I had no idea what he meant at the time.

The next morning, I woke up just before six o'clock, amazed I'd slept at all. Everything felt different. There was a hollow in the house. The silence was so... total. I didn't realise until that moment just how many little noises Betty used to make – snoring, snorting, flapping her ears and whistling.

I knew that Dolly would need feeding and would probably need a cuddle. I knew I needed to get up and make tea. Or something. Then, as soon as I had begun to crawl out of bed, I heard a tiny squeak. Dolly was normally silent unless she wanted food. Betty often made a high-pitched whistling noise at the bottom of the stairs to tell me that she was awake and that it was time for breakfast. Was Dolly all right? Had something happened to her? There was nothing to stop her climbing the stairs and being with me.

What I saw when I got to the top of the stairs took my breath away. Dolly was sitting at the bottom step in exactly the same way that Betty usually did. She was bolt upright with her tail curled around her feet neatly, waiting for me. I ran down to her, crying and laughing at the same time. She'd never done that before, ever. It made everything more bearable. I cuddled her and gave her some cat milk.

Once showered and dressed, I went downstairs again and Dolly was there just like before at the bottom step. She knew she was free to climb up the stairs. She didn't have to sit there. Was she choosing to copy Betty's habits? Were they communicating? If Betty could get through to me then why shouldn't she get through to Dolly too?

Whatever was going on, it really helped.

I'd been told the cremation would be at eleven o'clock so I decided I would go to the rabbit field and lie on the grass among the flowers. This way, I would be receptive to 'whatever may happen' and be able to take care of myself if nothing did. I also wanted to be alone with my grief, although I also knew I needed support. Fortunately, Ann was available and she agreed to drive me to the rabbit field and wait until I was ready to leave.

At the appointed time, she parked by the stile at the bottom of the field. Thanking her profusely, I went on alone, halfway up the hill, and sat down on my picnic blanket. I threw little bits of carrot into the long grass before lying down on my back, feeling tears trickle past my ears. The sky was cloudy with patches of blue. It was a lovely summer's day and the grass gave off an earthy, comforting smell; I could feel the warmth of the ground through the blanket. I was surrounded by buttercups.

Emotionally, though, I felt almost numb, which was a blessing.

Then, quite suddenly, I caught my breath as I began to feel a sense of playful happiness in the sky. It was exactly the same as when Timmy had died, as though there was a group of animals playing in the sunshine about twenty feet above me to my right. The sky at the top of the hill almost sparkled with a sense of fun and joy.

"I love you so much Betty," I said quietly. "And you, Timmy. I do hope you're both all right and that some of these weird things are real and not just my mind playing tricks."

As I lay there, gazing at the clouds, I noticed a tiny heart-shaped patch of blue and, despite my sadness, I smiled. Human beings are hardwired to create patterns out of chaos but knowing that didn't stop me enjoying that little blue heart. I took a picture with my phone, listening to the crisp, artificial shutter sound before the patch of blue grew larger, morphing into a wobbly circle.

I thought about Betty, about the crazy love we shared when she was a puppy, the deep love we shared when she was an adult and the look of love she gave when she put her paw in my hand that last day. I knew that our love would last forever. It was not static, not a memory, it was here and now and real, right in my heart.

The blue patch grew a little more, becoming ragged at the edges.

Dolly needed me now more than ever. She'd lost her playmate and canine protector. Was it enough, just being Dolly's 'mother'? Yes, of course. But I felt so hopeless and empty. I looked up into the growing patch of clear blue sky and whispered, "What am I here for, then? Apart from being here for Dolly?"

As soon as I'd said this, I felt a gentle pressure as though a pair of hands were cradling the top of my head. To my astonishment, the patch of sky above me suddenly filled with a golden light. It didn't hurt my eyes like the sun would have done. It wasn't the sun because that was far to my left and still hidden by cloud. Within the light, I had the sense of two radiant beings looking down at me. There were no clear details. It was as though the light was too bright to allow their faces to be seen clearly. They peered down at me through the gold, emanating great power. I held my breath and stared up at them in awe.

To make matters even more surreal, I received another of those mental messages, an instantaneous blast of concept, translated immediately into words in my head. The voice was the same powerful, guiding voice that I'd heard before when I met the shark and the snake.

"You know what you have to do."

There was almost the sense of a chuckle at the same time, a deep, compassionate, all-knowing chuckle of recognition and care.

I'd spent so many years dismissing religion and spirituality as wishful nonsense and now I was lying in a meadow with infinitely wise, all-powerful golden beings from on high sharing a joke with me. There was intelligence, deep wisdom, love and benevolence in the light, combined with mild indulgence. There was no sense of mawkishness or sentimentality. This golden light felt magnificent and terrifying. And I felt stupid because I truly didn't know what I had to do.

"Know this," said the light.

There was a sense of otherness in the delivery of the words. This wasn't Betty or Timmy or anyone I knew. This wasn't human. This

144

was pure wisdom and love. Glowing. Golden. Radiant. Telling me to know this – to see and understand the big picture. To understand and realise the light.

Then the gold returned to blue sky.

I lay there with my mouth open, stunned. What had just happened? My heart was thumping. What? Me, the perpetual sceptic, seeing and hearing angels? In the sky above the hill, I could still feel that sense of happiness and play from the animals.

I felt a shift, a true glimmer of hope.

I could see now what he meant when the Buddha said that craving, attachment and aversion create a lot of our suffering. I'd accepted a certain amount of spirituality but still lived in a state of confusion. If, on our little boats of life, we cling to the grasses on the bank in order to cope with a scary world (grasping/attachment) then we also avoid the acceptance of a wider truth (aversion) that may bring comfort. Still, the speed of the water and where it could take us is scary.

As I wandered back down the hill towards Ann, I thought about how different life would be if I knew, with absolute certainty, that I hadn't hallucinated that golden light.

TWELVE

Messages and Rainbows

Ann locked up her car and we went together to the top of the hill where we could see into the next valley. We sat down on the grass, listening to the birds singing and the cows munching in the next field. I didn't know where to start. She left a silence for a while and then laughed gently under her breath.

"This is amazing," she said.

"What is?" I was still staring at the golden light in my mind and wondering whether I had, in fact, seen angels.

"This view," she said. "When you asked me to support you this morning, I knew that you would be in emotional pain so I'd decided to take you up to the top of a particular hill, to a place where you might be able to get some perspective."

I had no idea what she was getting at so I let her continue. My mind was still playing the image of that light and that comment, 'Know this.' What did that mean? Become enlightened? Know God? Become a Bible-basher? Wear sandals and stand on the corner of the street shouting at the sinners? Or, maybe, simply meditate. Shift from

147

samsara to nirvana. Nothing small then. I hadn't even expected an answer!

"I looked on Street View in Google Maps," Ann continued, "to find a high point. The amazing thing is, this is the exact view that I chose but I'd planned to get to it from the opposite valley. I didn't know you could get here from this field."

"That's quite a coincidence," I said.

"Is it?" She glanced at me sideways.

I paused. It was one thing to write in my private diary, sharing my mental babble in a way no-one else could hear, but quite another thing to talk out loud. I took the risk and told her about the gold and the message. As I spoke, I felt more and more foolish but she simply nodded. It didn't seem to shake her particularly and, to my relief, she didn't laugh. She simply told me about Saint Paul on the road to Damascus and a life-changing, blinding light bringing him to his knees.

When I got home, I made some tea and cuddled Dolly. I was in a daze, feeling unhinged and disconnected from my normal world. I was in a new zone, one for which I had no rules or language. Part of me wanted to go back to my old, narrow-minded life where I feared death and believed no-one. If I were to start shedding my old skin, what new, vulnerable flesh might be revealed? Flesh that knew nothing for certain. Would this new world of messages and angels be more terrifying than the old?

But I knew I couldn't go back. My old view was dead. I knew it was now time for me to take a journey into the unknown and engage fully in a world I'd dismissed as nonsense for my entire adult life. The only way was forward.

I let Dolly out into the garden and watched her as she made her way across the grass to her little house. When I could see she was settled, I lay on the sofa and, feeling slightly foolish, tried to open my mind to the possibility of communication with Betty. I knew that, for Bill, this would just be a daily occurrence but for me it felt utterly weird. I closed my eyes. Then, not expecting anything to happen, I asked Betty how I could get through the next few months without her.

"You haven't finished your journey yet, Mummy. There are things you need to do." My eyes shot open. I knew it wasn't my subconscious because I would never use the word 'Mummy' when speaking to myself.

My mobile phone rang. It was Richard, one of my dear friends who'd helped at Timmy's funeral. He asked how I was and I told him that Dolly and I were surviving. As we talked, I felt light pressure on my head, the same as in the rabbit field. Then, to my total surprise, I felt Betty's front legs resting on me. I didn't know what to do and was too embarrassed to say anything to Richard. Even though he and I sometimes discussed theology, I felt embarrassed to share the far-out stuff. I could barely share it with myself.

It was so strange, lying there, feeling Betty lying on me. I knew that normally, if Betty were to lie on me like that, her weight would crush me but her spirit hardly weighed anything. I put my free hand up above me and felt something. The contact was feather-light.

Perhaps I should have been exclaiming to Richard like the prophets in the Bible or standing on the rooftop with my robes (and beard) whipped by the storms, my wild hair backlit by the setting sun. Instead, we quietly closed the conversation and I lay there smiling, feeling tears of love trickle down towards my ears as the contact with Betty slowly drifted away.

I had never believed in Heaven or Hell, yet I could see I'd created a personal Hell of spiritual darkness and isolation for over forty years. I didn't need to die to experience it. Just by ignoring the genuine experiences of others and the wisdom of realised teachers, I'd lived with a quiet, background terror for years. This fear was simply a projection of my own psyche, possibly caused by a trauma that I was yet to explore.

If somebody says something repeatedly with enough conviction, people begin to believe it. Unfortunately, as we have all experienced, this method is used in politics to very negative effect. Yet it's the same within our own minds. We all do this. We grab onto a concept, belief or life choice, for example, then we cling to it and refuse to explore an alternative viewpoint. We can decide something about our world and end up believing it to be true. It may even be true to start with but even if it changes over time, and we don't notice, it will stay as our fixed reality.

Imagine someone is living with a very ancient grandmother who, we firmly believe, will never give up her old, heavy teapot. She's a lovely lady but a bit stubborn. Maybe we don't want to cause an upset by suggesting teabags or a lighter pot. Besides, if she were to die just after we'd had an argument about the teapot, we'd never forgive ourselves. This is all a self-constructed reality. We suffer because, every single day, we have to carry this heavy teapot and it hurts our wrists. If we were to risk creating a gentle boundary for our own wellbeing, rather than having a push-pull argument, we may find that she is fully in agreement and that she never really liked that old teapot anyway.

I still had no idea what was real and what was imagination but what I did know was that I had to stop clinging to the bank and I had to follow this river without fear, wherever it was going to take me.

The next morning, Dolly was sitting at the foot of the stairs again, making her cute noises and I found myself chatting away to her like a crazy cat lady. It helped. I needed her so badly. Even with the amazing experiences I was having, it still hurt so much not having Betty physically with me.

I'd been sniffing Betty's enormous blanket bed a lot as it still held her wonderful autumnal, wolfish scent, but I needed to stop. I decided to fold the bed over. Dolly didn't take up that much space and I want to try to let go but, as soon as it was folded, I became uncomfortable with the idea that Betty couldn't lie on it like that. Of course she couldn't, you silly mare. Get a grip.

Then, out of the blue, I heard her voice again.

"My bed's more comfortable than you could possibly imagine."

I hadn't been trying to communicate. I hadn't been praying to the sky about my life purpose. I was just in confusion about what to do and I'd got an answer. So I decided to talk to Bill and John, to see what they thought of it all. Fortunately, they were in and I arrived at their house just as they were having coffee. Bill put his arms around me in welcome.

"How are you doing?" he said.

I burst into tears and heard him mutter "Stupid question" to himself. His grip on me was tight as though he could protect me from suffering by the pressure of his arms alone. Actually it was a bit too tight and I squeaked. He laughed and held me to his broad chest more gently, allowing me to cry.

"Sorry," he said. "I forgot about your poorly neck. I'm a silly old fart."

I laughed through my tears.

"It's like a wall when it hits you, isn't it?" I said, my voice muffled by his tee-shirt.

"Oh yes, it is," he said.

John put the kettle on and got another coffee cup out. RG, their big ginger cat, came in through the cat flap and I could feel him rubbing around my legs.

"Maaooow." His voice was much stronger than Dolly's quiet squeaks.

"RG's come to help," said John. "Say 'Hello' to Auntie Helen."

"Hello, RG."

"Maaooow."

I bent down to stroke him but he reminded me too much of Timmy. Bill enveloped me again.

"Maarrooow."

Finally, we settled round the table and I plucked up the courage to tell them what had been happening.

"I've had a few messages from Betty," I said.

"It reminds you," Bill said, nodding like it was all normal, "that even the greatest doubters, the people that would still argue that it's not real... it tells you it's not over."

"That some kind of life goes on?" He nodded again and asked how Dolly was coping. "She's been doing things that Betty used to do. She's almost half dog, half cat." They both smiled. "Over these last few years, she's gone from being terrified of everybody and everything," I continued, "into a fluffy cat who's looking after me, keeping me sane. I don't think Dolly can see Betty in the same way that Betty could see Timmy. Betty would look into empty space and track along the garden fence or on the sofa."

I needed this time. This wasn't just about grief, it was about trying to test new ideas in a safe place and their kitchen was a very safe place. I launched into my tale about seeing the gold colour in the sky and could see they were listening without judgement. It brought comfort to find that they talked quite rationally about it, agreeing that there's a whole bigger picture to be discovered about being human and what we all have to learn.

We talked about coincidence, about sensing animals after they've passed, and Bill shared how he could often feel Titch rubbing against his legs as he worked on the computer. I could feel a new confidence in the idea that I wasn't hallucinating all these wonderful things after all and that, if I spoke about these things, I wouldn't be rejected.

The next day, I went to pick up Betty's ashes. I wasn't sure I could do it but knew I had to. I'd prepared an area on a shelf next to Timmy's casket and placed some flowers nearby. It was after hours at the vet so there were no customers around.

"Have you seen her yet?" said the nurse at reception, quite matter-of-fact. I gaped at her.

"Pardon?"

"Have you seen Betty?"

I shook my head. I didn't know where to start. She went on to explain how her deceased cat would appear in the kitchen sometimes or in the garden and she always seemed contented. I told her that I'd not seen anything but that I'd heard little messages in my mind. I didn't want to tell her about the golden light and the angels because I still felt shy about that.

First Jon, then Bill, and now this lady all felt that it was completely normal to sense their deceased cats. And they didn't talk about it in special hushed tones. For them, it was normal life. Author Glynis Amy Allen, in her book *Furry Spirits*, tells many tales of connecting with animals after they've passed. She says in her introduction, "Be reassured that your pet's spirit certainly lives on after their passing, and that you can reach out and connect with them again."[8]

You may know how frightening it is when an animal runs away for a little while. Glynis, an hereditary medium, is able to find lost pets whether they're still alive or not. If there were no truth in spirit connection, then this would be impossible.

Perhaps the experience of sensing our pets is really pretty common but a lot of us don't talk about it because we don't want to be considered wacky. Many people feel their deceased dogs jumping on the bed or rattling their food bowls. It may not be long-term, but just enough to let us know that they're okay.

I now knew it was important for me to continue to talk about this. If I stayed in my own little world, writing my diary or talking to the

---

[8] Published by Local Legend

Dictaphone, there would be a danger of me going back into my dark way of thinking.

Our brains can grow new cells and shrink old ones, depending on their usage, and develop new connections in a process called neuroplasticity. If we have a certain train of thought, neurons connected to that thought grow stronger. If we imagine playing a piano for example, the motor neurons related to playing the piano will wire together and become more numerous, even if we don't actually touch a piano at all. Research has shown that simply imagining the act creates a change in brain structure in the area related to playing the piano. If that person stops imagining playing the piano then, over time, those neurons will shrink back to their original state.

It's exactly the same with our beliefs.

For me to take a new direction in my belief system, I was going to have to continue to talk to people and stay open, because my old thought patterns would be stronger than the new patterns and would lure me back. It's like walking through a forest. We can travel down a well-worn, wide pathway of a certain type of negative thinking, but creating a new path takes effort because it hasn't been explored yet. It may be narrow and choked with plants and tall grasses. We have to make a route through and, until we've walked that way many times, it will remain narrow. Our brains much prefer the old, well-trodden routes even if they bring us suffering.

If we suffer from anxiety, it's the same thing. Every time we allow ourselves to ruminate in anxiety, for example worrying about our pets' health or our mortality, those paths become wide and flat and, although terrifying, they're easy to walk down. Yet every time we sit down quietly with a trusted friend or in nature and allow ourselves to stay present, breathe and relax, we create a new pathway. One of peace. Continuous practice of this widens the peaceful pathway and the old anxious pathway gradually narrows down again as the unwanted neurons dwindle and fade. Eventually, our minds very rarely go down the anxious pathway and, if they do, we know how to step away onto the lovely wide path of peace quickly.

This is what I was referring to earlier about 'sewing your own parachute'. By creating pathways of peace and happiness in calm times of our lives, we have the resources and tools to deal with life when it gets rough.

Of course, in practice this is really tricky and it can take quite a long time to develop the new paths. It isn't a question of a quick meditation or prayer and everything turns out fine. Thankfully, I was to have many more spiritual experiences, all of which aided me in my journey to a new mindset.

But right now, as I was talking to the veterinary nurse and waiting to get Betty's ashes, my mind was in shock. All my calm resources had flown out of the window. I was ushered into a private room. First, the vet asked me how I was doing and I told her that I was surviving, but only just. I told her I wanted to hold back the tears until I'd got the ashes home.

"If I let go now," I said, "I won't be able to do it."

She nodded and looked me in the eye. She looked pale.

"Releasing Betty was the most difficult thing I've ever done in my career." She paused briefly as her comment slowly sank in. The most difficult thing. She would have put so many animals to sleep but my precious Betty had been the most painful loss. I tried to smile but my lips trembled and I couldn't speak. "Are you ready?" she said.

I wasn't, but I nodded. When the box was in my hands, I went numb. It was surprisingly heavy. White cardboard with a picture of a dove. Inside, was a neat casket with Betty's name inscribed on a brass plate. It didn't feel real and yet it was horribly real.

A few days later, I was taking my daily walk. It was sunny with a blue sky and lots of fluffy clouds. A beautiful summer's day yet I felt rubbish. I'd decided to go to the brambles where Betty and I had walked on that last day. I was just standing quietly, staying in the present moment and listening to the breeze in the trees and looking at the blackberry flowers, when I suddenly felt Betty's presence all around me. There was no mistaking it. I hadn't been wishing to feel her. It just happened.

I breathed quietly and enjoyed the feeling. Then I received a strong sense of gratitude from her. There were no words. I looked around wildly, breathing a quiet "You're welcome" to the trees. Looking up at the sky, I noticed a small section of rainbow between the fluffy summer clouds and simultaneously I heard a message in my mind.

"Try to be happy. The world is a beautiful place."

A mixture of sob and gasp escaped me. I could sense Betty so strongly. It was as though the whole sky had a wagging tail. I knew that this was not from my own mind – I would never have asked myself to admire the beauty of everything this early in the grief process.

I whispered, "I'll do my best" and continued walking through little alleyways and across patches of green until I reached the main road. That tiny patch of rainbow stayed in the sky as the clouds drifted and shifted. It wasn't the huge arc that I'd seen when Timmy died but the joy emanating from it was the same. And just like that earlier time, it came completely unexpectedly. I kept looking up and smiling.

When I got home, I gave Dolly a treat and went to the garden, hoping to see the last remnant of the rainbow. I gasped. It wasn't a small segment anymore, it had grown into an entire upside down rainbow, like an enormous multicoloured smile in the sky. I lay on the grass with Dolly, looking up. Then, two side arcs appeared, either side of the smile. Three tall, arching rainbows. A huge grin spread over my face, big enough to match the sky, and I felt relief flooding through me.

During this period, the national economy was plunging into financial crisis and the government was savagely cutting benefits to disabled people even if they needed and deserved them. It was a cruel cull. I still wasn't well enough to work and was totally reliant on benefits for everything. I owned the house but, if my money was stopped, I would have nothing to eat but the brickwork.

Friends said that the government surely wouldn't leave me without a safety net but it was already beginning to happen to others. Disabled people were becoming homeless and destitute, forced to rely on their families for survival. Some were even taking their own lives. My brother, my only family, was now living abroad and I was too sick to be able to travel to live near him. In order to survive independently for as long as possible, I decided to sell up, move to rented accommodation and cut back on my expenses. It was the only thing I could think of. Many people would have relied on the government but I didn't trust them to care for the sick anymore.

Many rental places were really expensive but I was able to find a cheap bungalow in a nearby suburb. The garden was a decent size and it had a big, south-facing living room. It was far posher than anything I could have bought. I could still get to the vet that I trusted and was still within reach of my friends. The only real difference was being beholden to a landlord's rules and whims. At least I knew I could manage financially for a few years from the sale of my house, even if the government stopped supporting me.

Dolly seemed happier in the new place because she didn't have to jump over the fence anymore. There was an old hedge at the back, the kind you see in a country field, all hawthorn and brambles, and she could get through it and explore to her heart's content without having to strain herself. She would disappear for hours and return smelling of horses, her fluffy tail and long pantaloons covered in grass seeds. This proved to be rather a problem because she still didn't like having her back end brushed and trying to get all these sticky seeds out was tricky. But it had to be done. I just told her it was the price to pay for roaming where there were hay bales and horses. I'd love to have known where she went. I didn't know anybody nearby who had a field of horses but maybe she was roaming quite a long way. For a thirteen year-old cat, she was doing very well.

Throughout that next year, she still took me by surprise in her Betty-like behaviour. She still said goodnight to me at bedtime before settling down on the sofa and liked to lie on Betty's bed by the fire. One day, she was sitting in one of her cardboard boxes in the garden and I was eating an apple under the tree. She was watching me intently, looking as though she wanted some.

"Dolly, you don't like apples," I said.

She blinked slowly and resumed her staring. Just for fun, when I'd finished, I threw the core across the garden just like I would have done for Betty. Dolly dashed out of her box, grabbed the apple in her teeth and ran back to me with it. I could almost see an imaginary doggy tail wagging. I threw it again and she ran for it, picking it up and bringing it back to me. She'd never done this before and had certainly never showed any interest in anything as disgustingly vegetarian as an apple. For a moment, it was as though the two animals were combined. I wanted to believe that Betty was still communicating via Dolly and I loved that little round cat even more than I thought possible.

On the first anniversary of Betty's death, I felt a change of view would be helpful so I decided to go to the local Buddhist retreat centre for a couple of days. This wasn't the same kind of place that I'd gone to in my younger days and it was a different group, but I knew they would welcome me and provide a place of quiet retreat.

The day before I went, I found myself looking for Betty, even though I knew it was silly. She'd always come with me on my holidays. Suddenly the song *Love Is All Around* came into my head, with the lyrics, "It's everywhere you go." I felt hugged all over. Was that my subconscious mind? I knew that Bill would have said it was a message. I wondered how long I would look for her, here on Earth. As the song went through my mind, I couldn't deny the warm, loving feeling I had.

Ann drove me to the centre and helped me get settled in my room. A little later, when I was exploring the grounds, I got a text from another friend saying, 'Lots of people send good wishes to Betty.' It made me smile. During the two days I was at the retreat, it poured with rain. I alternated between sitting in the meditation hall, reading impenetrable Buddhist texts, and walking around the grounds with my umbrella as the rain blatted down and the sky cried with me.

As it got close to six o'clock, the time when she had passed away the year before, I carried a carrot to the statue of 'the deer and the wheel' at the entrance to the centre. The cosmic Buddhist wheel with its iconic pair of deer, one lying down each side of the wheel, was one of those images that had always been strangely familiar to me. The Buddha had given a talk in a park one day and, among his audience, were some deer who had laid down and listened, rather like the ox and the ass in the Bethlehem stable. I felt like I'd seen this image many times before and it always made me feel calm.

I squatted down near the statue, feeling cold fingers of rain trickling down the back of my neck as giant redwoods dripped overhead. All around me, the grasses and the flowering rhododendrons drooped. I laid a carrot at the feet of the deer and wished Betty happiness, praying that she would be well cared for, well fed and have good playmates.

I thanked her for bringing me a love deeper than I'd felt in years – unconditional, total, loyal, trusting, childlike yet protective and fun.

Having dried off from the rain and settled in my room, I was astonished when the air suddenly filled with Betty's scent. I kept inhaling and sniffing until it went away. I felt so blessed that I was still getting these occasional visits.

THIRTEEN

The Power of Prayer

Thich Nhat Hahn's talks on the afterlife had left me feeling slightly uncomfortable. If we dissolve into another form immediately after death like a cloud turns to rain, how can we receive scents or sounds from our beloved dogs or messages from spirits? Then I had a sudden insight. I'd seen both Beryl and Timmy's souls fly free of their bodies in golden mist. That had looked similar to steam evaporating from water. Is that what he'd meant by his metaphor of a cloud turning to rain – the soul leaving the body?

I'd assumed he meant that we simply dissolve into our component atoms and that those elements then feed the earth and return as grass or trees, for example. But maybe I'd misunderstood. Yes, our physical bodies will either dissolve into the earth or be scattered in the ocean in a way that will feed the planet, but souls fly free. Do they change form and, if so, into what?

Hospice nurses report that it's common for people to be met by their deceased loved ones just before death. My father certainly saw people when he was about to die. That means there has to be memory after death, even if only for a while. If there really is a continuation of consciousness, and a recognition of our loved ones, then I suppose it's only logical that we could have past life memories.

I was once at a First World War exhibition in the city centre. A war camp had been put up with a tent and mannequins wearing uniforms were standing at ease. Billycans and helmets were strategically placed around the camp in a haphazard but realistic way. Visitors were allowed free access to touch anything and explore and, so far, it was merely an interesting exhibition.

But when I went up to a mannequin and felt the fabric of the uniform, I got what I can only describe as some kind of cinematic flashback. I was suddenly filled with horror. I was now a terrified young lad, wearing an itchy, heavy uniform. I felt sick and couldn't breathe. I let go of the fabric and was back once more into the hustle and bustle of market stalls and burgers and children. If someone had asked me to touch the uniform again, I would have refused. I had an equally strong aversion to the tent, the billycans and the gas masks. I had to find a quiet café and sit down for a moment. That was the first time I'd had some kind of flashback to a past English life. Most of my feelings of resonance with other cultures in history had been with China, Japan and Tibet.

So maybe we do remember a little, rather like when we wake from a dream. But what aspect of us is doing the remembering? Maybe when we're reborn, or even ascend to another level, we forget the details but something remains. It isn't our name or our job or our likes and dis-likes but something far deeper than that. I've come to believe that we all have an unnamed, genderless, unidentified and probably timeless self and many of us have had a glimpse of that part of us at moments of deep peace. Maybe it's when watching a sunset on a quiet clifftop or being transported by some sublime music. Just for a moment, we transcend our day-to-day identifications of job, name and gender, and for a moment we touch that deep, quiet space that is our true selves.

A few months later, I was to have a really powerful spiritual experience, one that shook me to my core. Just as with my vision of angels in the meadow, it took me completely by surprise and, like then, I knew it wasn't my imagination as I couldn't have dreamed it up in a million years.

I'd enrolled on a writing workshop at the local community centre. We'd been offered pictures to inspire us to write a story and, as I crossed the room to choose my image, I got a sudden and overwhelming sense of an old school friend of mine who'd passed away only a week before. I stopped in my tracks as I heard him call my name, his voice clearly recognisable in my mind.

Feeling utterly shaken, I retreated to the loo to have a quiet moment. There, I got a clearly worded message that he was unhappy. At first I panicked then I pulled myself together and told my friend how sorry I was. I said a few words in my head, wishing him to find peace, and a few seconds later he drifted away. The only way I could go back to the writing workshop was by pretending, for the moment, that nothing had happened. This temporarily worked and I was able to continue the session.

The next evening, I was taking a stroll. It was September and the leaves were fluttering down like deep orange butterflies in the streetlights. There was a slight chill to the air. Again, my friend's presence became palpable. This time I sensed him on my left, just above my shoulder, and again he voiced that same sense of confusion and distress. Before I could say anything, or try another faltering prayer, I sensed something just above my other shoulder. It held huge power, just as light-filled and awesome as the beings I'd seen in the sky at the rabbit field.

I stopped in my tracks. As my friend again expressed how lost he felt, the being on my right said, "You have a decision to make." I knew this wasn't related to me but to my friend. I repeated the concept in my mind, trying to relay the message from the angel to my friend, while at the same time trying to stay upright and not fall to my knees in shock. The angel, or whatever it was, seemed to be asking my friend to join it and choose that path of light. I guess the decision was made because both beings then slowly drifted upwards, meeting over my head, before floating away. I never heard from my friend again.

I was blown away. I'd been wanting proof that it wasn't all in my head but I wasn't expecting to become a psychic medium. This kind of religious or spiritual imagery wasn't in my world view. How far would this go? It felt exhilarating and scary at the same time.

There was a proper old-fashioned church near my new place with yew trees and a pointy spire. I decided to see what it was like. I was a bit nervous because I'd heard they were rather evangelical but I chose them because their services started late and I was lazy in the mornings now that I didn't have to get up to walk Betty. I really wasn't sure about the service at first but then there was a hymn with words that really caught my heart. Thoughts of my recent experience with my friend flooded back and I began to cry. Within minutes, I was surrounded by wonderful church ladies all giving me hugs and holding my hand.

To my own surprise, I went along the next week as well and listened as the vicar talked about the importance of doubt so I went up to him afterwards and introduced myself. We had a chat and he offered to come and bless my house. I'm really glad I accepted because we ended up having a rewarding theological conversation in which we compared Buddhism and Christianity and he told me about a growing movement of Christian Buddhists. He told me that he'd been in the army and had had a near-death experience that turned him to God.

Over the next few months, I went to his church and chatted to him whenever he had time. He was a really interesting man, having read the Qur'an and many other religious texts. He was just the right person for me to speak to and yet, just as with Tibetan Buddhism, I still didn't feel comfortable about joining up fully. I could never get answers that satisfied me about the crucifixion or the wrathful, jealous God of the Old Testament.

When I first went to church as a child, I prayed very earnestly, utterly believing that every word I said would be heard by some giant being in the sky. I prayed for peace. Then I became disillusioned and dropped any thought of prayer from my life for about forty years. I didn't pray because I didn't believe that anyone was listening.

Larry Dossey MD, author of *Healing Words: the Power of Prayer and the Practice of Medicine*,[9] writes about controlled and repeated experiments looking at the power of prayer on microbes. The growth rate of the bacteria was affected in a statistically significant way whilst, of course, placebo doesn't work on bacteria. Thich Nhat Hahn also wrote about prayer in his book *The Energy of Prayer*,[10] saying that the Divine is not separate from us. "God and we are of the same substance. Between God and us there is no discrimination, no separation."

Having done more research and reading, I was becoming more inclined to accept the power of prayer, although I still have difficulties with the concept. For example, when somebody prays for their friend's surgery to go well and it does, they may claim that God guided the surgeon's hands. Maybe it's just because I worked so long in the NHS, but I want the surgeon to get some credit too. I would want to say that the surgeon did a fantastic job of healing my friend, and I would accept – albeit reluctantly and begrudgingly, as it meant I would have to open my mind even more – that prayer might well have helped the outcome if offered in a sincere and loving way.

But what if we pray sincerely and lovingly and the surgery doesn't go well?

---

9 Published by Bravo Ltd
10 Published by Parallax Press

In terms of the efficacy of prayer, Thich Nhat Hahn is very clear when he says that prayer is only really effective when done in a state of loving mindfulness, surrender and acceptance. We shouldn't just put out requests for ourselves, like writing to Santa.

When Jon was living with me, we used to watch the TV programme *Charmed* a lot. The witches in the programme were not allowed to use magic for their own gain. When Jon and I wanted our lasagne to turn out nicely, we would wave our arms at the oven in jest, pretending to do a spooky spell to make the topping crispy but not burnt. But then we would tell ourselves off, saying that we mustn't do that because we were working for our own personal gain. It's important to keep a sense of humour about all these deep and meaningful things.

Unfortunately the British government didn't seem to understand the concept of loving kindness. Their cull of disabled people was continuing and I was the next victim. I knew it had nothing to do with my medical situation. I was just one of a quota that had to be deducted from the list of claimants so that the government could save money. I was in no shape to appeal or protest because I simply didn't have the mental or physical energy.

I was in a particularly bad way at the time. Not only was I suffering my usual aches and pains, electric shock sensations, tight fascia and so on, but I was beginning to suffer with my throat. I'd been chatting to my friend Russell one day and all of a sudden the front of my neck went into spasm. At night, it felt like I was choking and I was beginning to get visual disturbance as well. My physiotherapist told me to continue with gentle movements of my neck and to take things very easy.

Fortunately, about a year before, I'd won a writing competition to meet a literary agent and although she wasn't interested in the book I was presenting to her she was very kind about my chronic pain situation. She'd sent me a free copy of a book called *Mindfulness for Health* by Vidymala Burch and Danny Penman.[11] Some books come and go in our lives whilst others have a huge impact. This was one of those books. Mindfulness is based on Buddhist meditation and this book is all about how to use mindfulness to control pain and improve health.

Up to this point, I'd been regularly using the relaxation techniques my mother taught me when I was fifteen. At the time, I'd been getting a bit strung out about my O Level exams so she'd got me to lie down on the floor. She didn't tell me to relax, in fact her first instruction surprised me.

"Become aware of your right big toe."

I remember opening my eyes and looking at her questioningly. She simply nodded with a wise smile and talked me calmly, bit by bit, through my body, simply becoming aware of each part. Then we went back and repeated this with breathing relaxation for each area. This technique is now known as 'the body scan' and is a fundamental part of mindfulness training, although all these techniques are as old as the hills. By the end of that first session with my mother, I was like a jelly on the floor. It was life-changing and I sailed through my exams without anxiety.

Usually, when in pain, I would use my mother's relaxation techniques rather than meditation and they helped massively. In fact, my entire career as an Occupational Therapist had been based on these techniques and I'd spent my working life teaching stress management and relaxation.

Reading the book by Burch and Penman, I finally understood the connection between focusing and letting go. I learned the art of resting my mind very gently on my breath or on the area of pain – not focusing hard, yet holding that awareness with a soft mind. I also learned the

---

[11]   Published by Piatkus

art of letting things flow. Pain isn't the same from one minute to the next and nor is the breath or the way we grieve. I finally understood how to breathe without controlling it and how to concentrate without tensing up.

Thich Nhat Hahn talked about this too but I hadn't understood it at the time. In fact, the instructions of Burch and Penman helped me understand what Lama Chime Rinpoche had wanted me to do thirty years before. I finally got it. As they say, better late than never. I was now ready to approach Mahamudra. It's funny how things come full circle.

Some guided meditations start with words like, "Let's begin by settling into comfort. Let your face soften..." Well, if you've got nerve pain in your face, a stabbing pain in your back or something in your throat that feels like a razor blade, you can't settle into comfort. If you're grieving the loss of your dog or cat, you can't let your face soften. It's too much to ask. However, you can practise something called 'radical acceptance'. This means learning simply to sit with the pain as it is without trying to change it. It's what my mother did when she said, "Become aware of your big toe." She didn't say, "Relax your big toe."

The Buddha said that suffering can be caused by hanging onto the things we want, pushing away the things we don't want and avoiding anything nasty. So it's clear that physical or emotional pain can be made worse if we don't work with some level of acceptance. That doesn't mean putting up with intolerable music in a café by trying to accept it mindfully: we can ask someone to turn the volume down, or we can leave, and we can choose our café and our music. If we have control of the situation, we can make changes. But we can't control when and how grief or pain will hit us.

I began to find that my level of pain dropped down a bit some of the time and that was gold. Even if it doesn't work straight away, it's worth persevering. It can take weeks to learn these techniques. Yet for the first time in years I was gaining some control over my pain rather than simply taking strong medication. Of course, there are always days when we just can't meditate or function. There are days when everything gets too much and that still happens for me now.

Financially, I was now completely reliant on the money left over from the sale of my house four years earlier. I still had some left but it wasn't going to last long and I still had to pay to have help in the house because there were things I couldn't manage on my own. I realised I was going to have to find a cheaper way to live at some point but I was already renting at the lowest end of the scale.

Fortunately, I came across a mutual friend looking for a lodger. Her house was one street away from Richard's and about three bus stops from the centre of the city. I could have a social life without having to drive, cats were welcome, it was affordable long-term and I'd have company. Also, I wasn't expected to do any housework apart from taking care of my own room. I didn't hesitate long.

The move this time wasn't as devastating because a host of friends stepped up to the challenge. I was told to rest while my stuff was squeezed into my bedroom and places were found for my other furniture. Eventually, when everything was settled, Dolly came out from under my bed and sat on my office chair as though nothing had really changed. She seemed happy with the new garden where the grass was knee-high all the way to a tangle of shrubbery by the back fence. She still had her favourite oversized mug full of rainwater to drink from and a sunny patch by the shed to sunbathe.

I found the mindfulness techniques I'd learned really helpful in accepting the rapid changes in my life and was still sometimes able to bring my physical pain down a bit. I was glad I'd had time to practise because I was about to meet some very choppy water.

Late one night, I heard a few shouts in the street but I ignored them since this was near the city centre. In the morning, I woke up, fed

Dolly in my room and hauled on my dressing gown to go and make a cup of tea. Dolly followed me down the stairs, expecting to go into the garden as usual. As I got to the bottom of the stairs, I couldn't take in what I was seeing. The murky water covering the dining room carpet didn't seem quite right somehow. Then it dawned on me.

We were flooded.

There was nothing I could do but accept what had happened. I had no idea how much damage had been done, but all I could do was take a couple of deep breaths, stay as calm as possible and look after myself, my housemate and Dolly, who looked just as confused as me. Fretting about it wouldn't make the water go away. I went back upstairs to get my wellies. As I waded through the kitchen, the water came three-quarters of the way up my boots.

I opened the back door and that's when reality finally hit me. Our wheelie bins were floating down the garden and the pot that held my Perpetua rose was submerged. Stinking, brown water lapped against the shed and I realised that all my art supplies and board games would have been destroyed. I sloshed back through the kitchen and turned on the tap. Nothing. I switched on the kettle. Nothing. In the toilet, which was downstairs, foul water came all the way to the rim of the bowl. My facial nerve pain was kicking in and I needed a wee.

It's normal, when we have a bad experience, to imagine it getting worse. We can't help picturing the worst case scenario and of course our body gets stressed as a result and our pain, whether physical or emotional, gets harder to bear. As stress levels rise, our fear of the future gets stronger and so it goes round in a vicious cycle. Our minds want to explore the future in order to prepare us. But if it keeps happening, we end up spending our lives in this terrible future as opposed to the difficult present.

Yet the opposite is also true. If we can catch ourselves just as we plunge into catastrophic thinking and bring ourselves back to the here and now, it's possible to save ourselves a lot of unnecessary mental anguish. It's a tricky thing to do.

We also tend to look back at the past and remember all the bad things that have happened. Again, this is perfectly normal, it's what our brains are programmed to do. It's just biology and yet it's painful.

When we notice we're remembering all our past hurts and griefs, maybe it's time to take a deep breath and, with great kindness towards ourselves, accept our pain and move gently back to the present moment. Decide on something kind and loving that we can do for ourselves to stay grounded, such as call a friend, smell some roses or make a cup of tea. It's not helpful to live in the past or the future and it takes quite a bit of skill to stay in the present. All we can do is our best.

Since there was no water, I couldn't have a wash or a drink so I went to Richard's house for breakfast. When I came back, the burst water main had reduced from a torrent to a stream and water company staff were marching up and down with clipboards. Volunteers were helping where they could.

Over the next few days, insurance was discussed, our damaged furniture was removed and men in official jackets sprayed everything to prevent cholera. The carpets had been removed and the concrete floors were damp. We had no washing machine and the place stank of old drains.

Thankfully, the Perpetua rose was fine once it had been rescued and placed upright near the shed although, as predicted, my art supplies and board games were ruined. Despite all this calamity, Dolly began to explore the garden once more, giving the world baleful, disapproving looks because her sunny spot was now covered in sludge and the grass was soggy.

Three weeks later, Dolly got sick. She didn't seem to be too unhappy but since she wasn't getting better as I'd hoped, I took her to a vet. My usual practice had moved location to a place too far away so I had to go to a huge shop that looked like a supermarket, selling dog and cat food, animal treats and toys, and offering small animals for sale. At the back of this was a veterinary surgery. When the vet examined Dolly, she frowned.

"I'm very sorry," she said. These are not words we want to hear from a vet or a doctor. "I've found a lump," she continued.

My world went white. It was as though someone had filled the room with fog. My guts clenched as my brain tried to understand what she'd just said. A lump?

"I'll do everything I can for her pain relief," she continued, "but I'm afraid she may only have two months left."

Two months?

I couldn't comprehend it. Because Timmy had lived so long, I had assumed Dolly would do so as well. She was only fourteen. I stroked her ears while the vet gave her a painkilling injection and handed me some tablets.

"These should keep her completely comfortable for the rest of her days and, if she lives longer than that, you can come back for some more."

Her lifespan was being measured out in tablets. Once again, I had to accept the unacceptable. I was losing Dolly. Everything seemed to be falling apart. I tried to stay in the present moment and enjoy her company while she was with me, but it's hard to stop the mind rushing to the awful truth.

We had a happy two weeks as Dolly sunbathed and enjoyed the soggy garden and I tried not to worry. She did so well that I began to relax into the idea that we would have a spring together after all. However, one evening, it was clear to me that something was very, very wrong. She came wobbling towards me and lay at my feet, looking up at me as though asking for help.

Part of my mind was running around panicking but thankfully another part of it stayed calm. I picked her up to see if she could stand on her own and was horrified to find that she couldn't. Her head was tipped on one side, too, just like Betty's had been and I knew she'd reached her journey's end. I couldn't let her suffer.

"Oh, Dolly, I'm so sorry," I whispered. "I'm so sorry."

There was no doubt.

FOURTEEN

The Caterpillar and The Butterfly

Fortunately, the vet was able to come to the house straight away. It was around this time, when Betty had passed, that my favourite vet and nurse had been holding me, crying and hugging and talking about how wonderful Betty had been. Sadly, I didn't know this vet. When the dreadful task was done, she left me alone to grieve.

I knelt on the ground by the bed and buried my face in Dolly's fur. She'd gone, quietly and gently, just like she'd lived her life. This time I hadn't seen her spirit leave her body, nor did I have another animal companion to remind me that something continues after death. I was alone in a flooded house with the body of my dear friend.

It was at this bleak moment that I noticed a subtle golden glow, almost like a cloud, above the bed. I glanced up to see whether the ceiling light had been left on. It was off. Was this Dolly? Was it an angel?

It's somehow easy to be compassionate towards other people and much harder to give ourselves the same care and attention. We need to learn to give ourselves the same love we would give to a dear friend. If we can learn to accept the things we cannot control and treat ourselves with compassion, our little boat of life is less likely to capsize. No-one can stop the waves or the rocks, but we can learn to navigate the river and can develop a sturdy little boat that doesn't tip over at the first wave. Even when the wave is a tsunami of grief, the boat will rock and it may even fall to the side, but with mindfulness techniques we can come back up.

I remembered Lama Chime Rinpoche telling me not to get bogged down in books or ritual but to focus on the here and now and use any activity as a meditation. Could I stay here with my beautiful friend and be kind to myself by paying attention to how I felt rather than trying to run away? Could I enter a state of meditation?

I became aware of my breath, the sensation of Dolly's fur against my fingers and the soft light above me. To my surprise, instead of the expected collapse into emotional agony, I felt a wave of love surrounding and filling me. This may sound totally bonkers, but it seemed as though Dolly, instead of flying away, had decided to stay and was curling up deep in my heart. I could feel a warm, velvet affection in my chest. I put one hand on my heart and one hand on Dolly and wept, but this time did not feel alone. This time, there was a mixture of grief and intense, unconditional love.

The light had gone when I looked up. I was to learn later, when I studied near-death experiences, that a temporary golden light is often seen as people pass. So why not with animals? After all, humans are animals. We just pretend we're superior.

I couldn't stay in the present moment anymore. The past called me. I held Dolly's paw and thought about her life and how brave she'd been, about how she'd learned to trust people and to love Betty. She'd led a poetic life, a true hero's journey. To watch a creature transform from a state of terror and distrust, frightened by the trauma of her youth, into this loving, trusting being who had continued to grow in confidence right up to her last few moments, was miraculous. She'd learned how to manage her fear and as a result had lived a warm and loving life. It was sad that the ending had been so rushed yet I was glad that there'd been time to say farewell.

I gently placed her on her favourite chair, tucked her up as if for sleep in a warm blanket and went to bed. As I lay there, trying to sleep, I remembered how bedraggled her fur had been when she first arrived at my house and how terrified her big round eyes had been as they peered at me from under the bed. I remembered her escape and how I had then held out the blanket for her to jump into my arms. That's when our hearts first connected. Now, I could feel her in a palpable way. It was like sharing the inside of my chest with a warm, brown teddy bear. Her love was within me, part of me.

I'm not quite sure how I managed to sleep that night but, when I woke, reality hit me hard. I forced myself out of bed, had a quick shower and threw on some clothes. I didn't care what I looked like. I placed Dolly on her blanket in a cardboard box and added some flowers from the garden and a poem of love. The bedraggled red mouse – the one she'd had with her under the shed when she was afraid and alone all those years ago, and that had been by her side every day since she'd come to live with me – I now laid gently between her paws one final time.

We all go through life with some kind of coat, whether it's made of fur, skin or feathers. When it's time to leave, we take off our coat and leave it behind as we go on our journey. If we're fortunate, those who love us take good care of our coat, treating it with respect. But at that point, that's all it is. It's a beautiful garment that housed our soul. Our loved ones are not being cremated or buried. They have long since flown. We are simply dealing with the coat that's been left behind.

Even though I now knew this, I still had to tear myself away from her at the vet's. I still felt like I was leaving her behind. Some lessons take a long time to learn.

Later, I took an evening walk. Cherry trees were bursting into froths of pink. I looked up at the deep blue evening sky through the blossoms, feeling cheated that the universe could be so beautiful when I felt so rubbish. Then I thought about how nature goes to sleep in the winter and wakes up in spring. The circle of life. I saw that the beauty all around me was not an insult to Dolly's passing but a reminder that maybe Dolly was now as fresh and new as the blossom above me. Sun after rain. Life after death. Whatever the truth of it all, it was a far nicer thought than feeling betrayed by nature.

The next day, I went to visit Bill and John, hoping for comfort. I wasn't disappointed. They were towers of strength and helped me through a few hours while their cats made me smile too. As I got into my car to leave, I glanced over at Bill standing by the front door and looking a little tearful.

"You know," he said, "Dolly isn't going anywhere. She'll be with you for the rest of your life."

Somehow, he knew. I hadn't told him about the feeling of her joining me and curling up in my heart. I could still feel her there, a warm, comforting presence and I smiled. I could see from Bill's sadness just how much he'd loved her.

Weeks later, our house was still wet through. All the carpets had been removed and we were still walking around on wet concrete. Although my housemate and I had accepted a meagre amount of insurance compensation, the landlord had done nothing about fixing the problems. Black mould was growing at treble its normal rate. The house was a hellhole. I was miserable. And once more, I had to escape.

I chose a bungalow that allowed pets, twenty minutes from the city. My heart was still shattered at the loss of Dolly and I couldn't see myself having another animal so soon but at least I would have the opportunity in the future. I hadn't got rid of Dolly's things, I didn't have the heart. I just cleaned everything and kept the crate of cat food in the garage.

I survived the move quite well but, a few months later, my pain flared up in a way it never had before. It was caused mainly by a new physiotherapist whose exercises proved too much for my dysfunctional body. My fascia tightened from my foot to my neck, severely affecting my ability to speak and swallow. When the pain hit, it was like having a razor blade in my throat. I could no longer sing and could only speak softly.

Two things made this nightmare a little easier to bear. The first was the presence of a myofascial therapist, and it was nothing short of a miracle that his office was just a few doors down from my house. The second was the idea of starting a new writing project, a book about my pets. I wanted to share the story of my animals and how they'd changed me. I thought it might help me cope with my current situation and, maybe, my journey could be of help to someone else one day.

As I began reading my old diaries and listening to my Dictaphone recordings, I felt a renewed faith that there really was a bigger picture and that all creatures go on to experience something further after death. This gave me strength.

Actually, there was a third thing that helped, becoming a cat foster mother. Over time, my throat and body pain gradually got a little easier although I was still unable to drive or walk more than a few yards. When a friend asked me to look after a tiny, black cat called Snib for a couple of weeks I was delighted, although I felt a little nervous about whether I'd be able to cope physically. I was happy that I'd kept Dolly's food and toys. They now had a good purpose.

Snib provided me with cuddles and entertainment whilst I, in return, fed and nurtured her. I found myself smiling again for the first time in months as Snib snuggled into my armpit for a cuddle. Having her to stay was absolutely worth it, even though I had to limp down to the therapist when my lower back gave out.

A few weeks after Snib had gone back to her parents, I met Kuro. I'd been tagged on Facebook by somebody as a potential cat foster mother and a young woman needed me to look after her cat while she was in temporary accommodation. Once he was out of his carrier, Kuro came over to me and nudged my hand with his face.

"That's good," said his owner, Danielle. "He likes you."

"He's cute."

"He gets wonky days," she said. "His head tips on one side but he soon gets better. I've got medicine for him and I'll be around to help if you can't manage."

She said she would pay all the bills and take him to the vet if he needed it so it was the best of both worlds. He was a delightful little chap. When he had his wonky days, I would make sure I was quiet around him. Sometimes, we had wonky days together where we just lay in bed. When we were both well, we went out into the garden to explore the flowers. After five months, Danielle bought a house in the city and it was time for Kuro to go to his forever home.

Then, in mid-August, the bird hit the window and my heart failed. The ambulance hurtled along the road, blue lights flashing, sirens screaming. I was close to death. It was finally my turn.

Instead of panicking, I thought back to everything that had happened. Beryl and Timmy had flown away from their bodies in golden mist, there was that zephyr of peaceful wind in the park from my aunt and the dream visit from my uncle saying goodbye. I'd had clairvoyant dreams, the sense of Betty after she passed and received all those little messages in my mind. I remembered the beings of golden light and how Dolly looked after me when I thought I couldn't cope. Finally, there was the light above the bed and the feeling of her entering my heart. All these thoughts gave me courage after a lifetime of fear.

I knew that I needed to stay calm and accept what was happening. Fortunately, I had time to pray so I asked whoever might be listening to let me live so that I could finish my book; but I added that if I were supposed to die, then please would God or Source or Love take me into their arms and care for me.

I was in full acceptance of what was happening and meant every word. As we hurtled down the A52, I repeated my prayer over and over like a mantra: "Please let me live, but if I am to die, please take me in your arms."

Focusing on light and hope at the end of life is something everyone can do and, according to the Buddhist tradition, it really helps our future. Whatever you believe though, it has to be a better way to go than panicking. For so many years I had honestly believed that my potential point of death was going to be filled with horror. But through regular meditation practice, or at least some attempts, I was able to catch that moment and redirect my mind towards the light. And due to my animals, there was indeed light to believe in. I only hope that when my next time comes, I can do the same.

I hope the same for everyone.

Thankfully, I lived, but my heart was in serious trouble. The consultant leaned over me on the freezing slab of the angiogram table.

"You have a rare heart condition," he said. "It's called Takotsubo Cardiomyopathy. A failure of the left ventricle, often caused by stress."

The two years of being housebound and in chronic pain coupled with all the personal losses had been too much for me. I was admitted to the coronary care unit (CCU). Ann arrived with a carrier bag of useful things like pyjamas, orange juice and hand wipes. Jon the singer came in next carrying Lemmy, a stuffed toy lion I'd made forty years before and who travelled everywhere with me. Richard, Russell, Danielle and other dear friends visited and kept me company. I had a caring phone call with Tony, my first love, and his mother, and my brother and his wife travelled down from Scotland to be with me.

"I hope you realise," said Jon quietly, leaning forward, "how much your family love you."

Tears sprang to my eye. He meant that my friends were my family too and that, although I now had no animals and would be unlikely to have any more in the near future, I was surrounded by love. I was not alone.

After three days, I was transferred to a ward. From there, I found myself discharged with a bucket of pills and ensconced on the floor of a friend's house because the doctors weren't keen for me to go back to the bungalow on my own. My condition was known to have a risk of recurring and I would have been too far from the hospital for safety.

It was a wise decision. Three days after being discharged it happened again. I managed to stagger to the front door to unlock it, lie down and call an ambulance. More flashing blue lights and screaming sirens. I felt more afraid this time yet, once more, was able to bring to mind the golden beings in the rabbit field and all the other evidence of a bigger picture.

Over the next two years, I was admitted to hospital thirteen more times with chest pain caused by the rare Printzmetal angina, or coronary spasm, which had come about as a result of my heart failure. I was told it could occur when under stress or even when at rest. An infection or getting too cold could trigger it and, each time, I would be in danger of a potential heart attack. I was put on strong medication to keep everything as stable as possible and increase my chances of living a long life without further incident.

But basically, I could drop down dead at any moment.

I couldn't go back to my old bungalow because I needed to live near the hospital, so I found a second floor retirement flat in the city. I had no garden of my own, wasn't allowed pets and the flat was on a noisy main road. Although it was a far cry from the life I'd hoped for, I was grateful to be alive. Jon said he would keep my Perpetua rose in his garden until I got a better place to live. One day, I hope to plant the rose in a garden of my own and let its scented blossoms spread across a wall or fence. I hope to have a peaceful and quiet place to live with new animal friends. This still remains a dream.

Meditation, especially on compassion and acceptance, has kept me in the present moment for the most part and eased any catastrophic thinking. However, the main reason I was able to cope without freaking out completely was my animals. Without their visions and messages, I believe I might have continued to dismiss the evidence from humans as wishful thinking and fantasy. Because of everything these loving animals had shown me, their gifts beyond price, I'd been able to open my mind to further spiritual experiences. And I now had evidence for the existence of the peace that passes all understanding. For the rest of my life, no matter how long or short, I want:

❖ to be gentle like Timmy, relaxing in the sun and bringing comfort to others,

❖ to bounce through the buttercups of life like Betty, embracing each moment,

❖ and to trust in the love of the universe, just as Dolly trusted in me.

Do I now believe in God? Certainly not the God I was told about as a child, the wrathful, bearded, judgemental chap sitting on a cloud and dooming everyone to Hell. However, whilst not ready to turn into a bright-eyed convert to anything in particular, I am now open-minded about the spiritual world and happy to explore its various religions and beliefs.

I have come to believe that the fundamental nature of the majority of sentient beings is good. We are all part of an interconnected whole in which we are interdependent with everyone and everything, connected to one another, and that life is about becoming aware of this and seeing the wider view.

Due to the Internet, we now have access to evidence from all around the world and from history of a spiritual dimension to reality: spirit communication beyond death, near-death experiences of light and love and people able to sense extraordinary things. Our minds are far more powerful than we have ever suspected.

Yes, I still have moments of doubt. My old, habitual fears often return in the night when my heart cramps in pain. Our thought patterns don't change in the blink of an eye. Sometimes it takes time and effort to change our inner landscape. The difference between my younger days, when I was overwhelmed by a fear of death, and my being now, is that I have beautiful experiences to call upon, experiences that bring me hope and courage.

> *To be or not to be? That is the question…*
> *To die, to sleep.*
> *To sleep, perchance to dream: ay, there's the rub.*
> *For in that sleep of death what dreams may come…*[12]

Just as the caterpillar has no concept of the butterfly, none of us knows exactly what 'sleep of death' awaits us. Yet the evidence is out there that we'll meet again those we have loved, including our pets. So what should we do with this awareness? Should we simply carry on with a smile and face our mortality with a less tremulous heart, or should we

---

[12]   Hamlet, Act 3, Scene 1 (William Shakespeare)

go further? How would people's lives be different if we knew for certain that our actions had consequences beyond this life?

It's now clear that we must learn to treat all creatures with respect and love, including those deep under the sea and on the highest mountain. The number of animals joining the 'sentient' list grows every year. Every soul on this planet, whether covered in skin or fur, is worthy of love and care. It seems highly likely that each being contains a golden mist that travels onwards somewhere, guided by angels to a place of joy.

And wouldn't it be wonderful if humanity could grow up as a species and become kind?

Postscript

As I was finishing the writing of this book, Tony's mother Pat passed away at the age of ninety-seven. She was my dear friend and a mother figure to me for over thirty years after my own mother died. I hadn't seen her for a long time due to my inability to travel, but we'd kept in touch on the phone and with letters.

As soon as I received the awful news from Tony, I was able to contact Lama Chine Rinpoche and he immediately started saying prayers for her. I now believe that those prayers mean something and that the prayers said for my mother by the Dalai Lama meant something too. They have purpose and effect. Prayer has now become a part of my life.

This recent unhappy experience shows me how much I've changed over the years. My grief used to be all about ME and my sadness was all about how unfair death was, how I had lost this person or animal and how this had affected my life. Perhaps I can't be blamed for this self-interested approach because it's natural and normal. But having a wider belief system now has changed how grief feels. Yes, there is still the terrible pain of loss, yet my experiences have allowed me to hope that Pat is in her prime again, recovering from life in this world and meeting all the dear ones lost to her through the years.

I would love to think that she will, one day, look down on me as I hold this book in my hands, proud of my attempt to bring some kind of reassurance to the world. This book may only be one little drop of care in the ocean of human troubles, but without these little drops there is very little hope for our spiritual wellbeing.

Each drop, from each one of us, really counts. Whether it's sending flowers to someone who is feeling sad or campaigning against injustice, it all helps. Everyone, whether clothed in skin or fur, can make a difference in the world.

If you have enjoyed this book...

Local Legend is committed to publishing the very best spiritual writing, both fiction and non-fiction. You may also enjoy:

SPINACH SOUP FOR THE WALLS
Lynne Harkes (ISBN 978-1-907203-46-6)

This is a message of hope for anyone in despair and a call to see our troubles as opportunities for growth. Lynne had a privileged life in wonderful and colourful places, from South America to Africa, and she tells us of the magnificent natural world there and the resilience of its people. Yet she found herself retreating into isolation and unhappiness, out of touch with spirituality. This is the story of how she learned to "recognise the remarkable in the ordinary", rediscovering herself and a new way of being.

Winner of a Gold Medal in the national *Wishing Shelf Book Awards*.
"...a spiritually rewarding book... Highly recommended."

FURRY SPIRITS
Glynis Amy Allen (ISBN 978-1-910027-48-6)

The loss of a pet can be devastating. They have been members of our family, unconditionally loving and much more than 'a furry friend'. We need to know whether they live on and can perhaps communicate with us. This wonderful page-turning book, by a bestselling author and hereditary medium, has the answers and much more. In everyday language and often with humour, Glynis gives fascinating and evidential stories of animal survival as well as describing the amazing healing and psychic abilities of animals.

GHOSTS OF THE NHS

Glynis Amy Allen (ISBN 978-1-910027-34-9)

It is rare to find an account of interaction with the spirit world that is so wonderfully down-to-earth! The author simply gives us one extraordinary true story after another, as entertaining as they are evidential. Glynis worked for thirty years as a senior hospital nurse in the National Health Service, mostly in A&E wards. Almost on a daily basis, she would see patients' souls leave their bodies escorted by spirit relatives or find herself working alongside spirit doctors – not to mention the Grey Lady, a frequent ethereal visitor! A unique contribution to our understanding of life, this book was an immediate bestseller.

Winner of the SILVER MEDAL in the national *Wishing Shelf Awards*.

"What a fascinating read. The author has a way of putting across a story that is compelling and honest… highly recommended!"

THE QUIRKY MEDIUM

Alison Wynne-Ryder (ISBN 978-1-907203-47-3)

Alison is the co-host of the TV show *Rescue Mediums*, in which she puts herself in real danger to free homes of lost and often malicious spirits. Yet she is a most reluctant medium, afraid of ghosts! This is her amazing and often very funny autobiography, taking us back stage of the television production as well as describing how she came to discover the psychic gifts that have brought her an international following.

Winner of the Silver Medal in the national *Wishing Shelf Book Awards*.

"Almost impossible to put down."

SPIRIT SHOWS THE WAY
Pam Brittan (ISBN 978-1-910027-28-8)

A clairvoyant medium for over thirty years and highly respected throughout the UK, Pam describes herself as "an ordinary woman with an extraordinary gift." Despite many personal difficulties, she has shared this gift tirelessly and brought comfort and understanding of the Spirit to a great many people. Here, she inspires us to realise our own innate gifts and to trust that Spirit will always guide us on the right path.

AURA CHILD
A I Kaymen (ISBN 978-1-907203-71-8)

One of the most astonishing books ever written, telling the true story of a genuine Indigo child. Genevieve grew up in a normal London family but from an early age realised that she had very special spiritual and psychic gifts. She saw the energy fields around living things, read people's thoughts and even found herself slipping through time and able to converse with the spirits of those who had lived in her neighbourhood. This is an uplifting and inspiring book for what it tells us about the nature of our minds.

5P1RIT R3V3L4T1ON5
Nigel Peace (ISBN 978-1-907203-14-5)

With descriptions of more than a hundred proven prophetic dreams and many more everyday synchronicities, the author shows us that, without doubt, we can know the future and that everyone can receive genuine spiritual guidance for our lives' challenges. World-renowned biologist Dr Rupert Sheldrake has endorsed this book as "...vivid and fascinating... pioneering research..."

A national runner-up in *The People's Book Prize* awards.

A MESSAGE FROM SOURCE

Grace Gabriella Puskas (ISBN 978-1-910027-00-4)

Beautiful and inspiring poetry of the Spirit that reaches deep within the consciousness, awakening the reader to higher states of awareness, spiritual connection and love. The author, in familiar and thoughtful language, explores the power of meditation, the nature of the universe and of time, our place within the environment and who we truly are as creative beings of light and sound.

Winner of the Local Legend national *Spiritual Writing Competition*.

THE HOUSE OF BEING

Peter Walker (ISBN 978-1-910027-26-4)

Acutely observed verse by a master of his craft, showing us the mind, the body and the soul of what it is to be human in this glorious natural world. A linguist and a priest, the author takes us deep beneath the surface of life and writes with sensitivity, compassion and often with searing wit and self-deprecation. This is a collection the reader will return to again and again.

A winner of our national *Spiritual Writing Competition*.

ODD DAYS OF HEAVEN

Sandra Bray (ISBN 978-1-910027-17-2)

If you feel that you've lost the joy in your life and are not sure where you're going, this book is written for you. Sandra knows those feelings all too well. Rocked by mid-life events, she refused to be a 'victim' of circumstances and instead resolved to treat them as opportunities for change and growth. She looked for a spiritual 'guidebook' to offer her new thoughts and activities for each day, but couldn't find one – so she wrote it! In this book, and her sequel *Even More Days of Heaven*, we find hundreds of brilliantly researched suggestions, sure to life our spirits.

Runner-up in the Local Legend national *Spiritual Writing Competition*.

Local Legend titles are available as paperbacks and eBooks.
Further details and extracts of these and many
other beautiful books for the Mind, Body and Spirit
may be seen at
www.local-legend.co.uk

CPSIA information can be obtained
at www.ICGtesting.com
Printed in the USA
BVHW062152041122
651178BV00011B/1177

9 781910 027516